TALL TRUTHS
FROM
SHORT STORIES

CRATE H. JONES

BROADMAN PRESS
Nashville, Tennessee

4257-29
ISBN: 0-8054-5729-1

Dewey Decimal Classification: 248.6
Subject Headings: STEWARDSHIP // CHRISTIAN LIFE
Library of Congress Catalog Card Number: 87-11738
Printed in the United States of America

Library of Congress Cataloging-in-Publication Data

Jones, Crate H.
   Tall truths from short stories.

   1. Christian life—1960-   . 2. Meditations.
I. Title.
BV4515.2.J58   1987   248'.6   87-11738
ISBN 0-8054-5729-1 (pbk.)

To the Children—
Cathy,
Hannah,
Mark, and
Russell

Our "Heritage of the Lord"
(Ps. 127:3)

Foreword

I was sitting on the ledge in front of our house reading Crate Jones's first book *Out of the Crate* and found myself laughing—something I rarely do when reading.

But the stories were told with such wry humor, wit, and wisdom, I found myself applying them prayerfully to my own spiritual life.

Then to my delight along came *Tall Truths from Short Stories*. Equally as enjoyable as *Out of the Crate*—equally as inspiring and applicable.

The Bible says, "A merry heart doeth good. . . ." God blessed Crate Jones with a merry heart, and this book shows just how much good that merry heart can do you.

I recommend it enthusiastically.

RUTH B. GRAHAM

A Word from . . .

Crate Jones is a worthy member of the writing tribe. He has a gift for matching the right word to the right thought. I get manuscripts from aspiring writers and am convinced that some who could write won't and others who can't write try. Crate has something to say and says it well. He follows the pattern in Holy Writ: "The words of the wise are as goads, their collected sayings like firmly embedded nails, given by one Shepherd" (Eccl.12:11, NIV).

THE LATE VANCE HAVNER

Crate Jones has a memorable and novel way of sharing stories. The reader runs the gamut of emotions from amusement to sympathy to sadness. His ability to so touch the emotions is keenly used to convey vital spiritual principles. I commend this volume to you with excitement.

JACK R. TAYLOR

You will be rewarded for every minute that you spend on the pages of this book. Crate Jones knows how to identify with what the majority of Americans feel but few can express. Perhaps that is why we all enjoy reading his poignant and refreshing stories . . . stories which magnify the best things in time and eternity.

W. A. CRISWELL
First Baptist Church
Dallas, Texas

Author's Preface

Tall Truths from Short Stories is a sequel to my first book, *Out of the Crate*. Based on true events, most of the stories are seen through the eyes of humor. All have an application to everyday situations.

Indebtedness is acknowledged for the help that has come in the making of this book.

First, to the Lord, without Whom there would be nothing. To Harriett, my helpful helpmate. To Eunice Austin, church secretary and tireless typist. To the good people of Angier Avenue Baptist Church for superior support. To Ruth Graham for her enthusiastic encouragement. And to Broadman Press for publishing and promotion.

With a prayer that the Lord will be pleased to bless this work, it is sent on its way.

CRATE JONES

Acknowledgments

The author wishes to thank *The Baptist Program*, published by the Executive Committee of the Southern Baptist Convention, for allowing him to reprint his articles, "Straight Shootin' on Stewardship" (from June-July 1984 issue), "Fresh Wind for Stewardship Sails" (September 1985), and "Trail of a Tither's Testimony" (August 1987); also for permission to reprint his articles from the Baptist Bulletin Service, "A Stone Unturned" (11-8-81) and "A Stingy Recollection" (7-17-83).

Unless otherwise indicated, all Scripture quotations are from the King James Version of the Bible. Those marked (NASB) are from the *New American Standard Bible*. Copyright © The Lockman Foundation, 1960, 1962, 1963, 1968, 1971, 1972, 1973, 1975, 1977. Used by permission. Those marked (NIV) are from HOLY BIBLE *New International Version*, copyright © 1978, New York Bible Society. Used by permission.

Contents

1
Tall Truths from . . .
A Word Fitly Spoken

Hell's Down—Heaven's Up

A Baptist preacher from New York was heading toward his new duties in the South. En route, he was introduced as a reverend to a man he would see only briefly. One of those questions designed to discredit the Bible and fluster the preacher came forth: "You a preacher? Tell me, where is hell?" It's real doubtful that the inquiree was trying to locate the place or the way to get there. More than likely he was saying, "If you can't tell me where it is, it ain't there."

Time being short, debate or argument would've been about as effective as trying to unlock a door with the wrong key. The subject was hot, but the preacher wanted to reply helpfully, with more light than heat. "Friend," he said, "I'm not traveling in that direction. If I meet someone who is, I'll try to get an answer for you." I wouldn't be surprised if that didn't burn some truth into the skeptic's head. It affirmed hell as real, and he was saying that some folks are not going there and some are.

Now the flaming truth is hell begins in a person's heart. Some live in it, raise it, create it for others, punctuate with it, and seem to think it a proper place for others to go. For a place that's nonexistent in the doubter's mind, its acrid smoke sure has smogged up the world.

Without trying to locate hell geographically, its direction is down. Peter said, "God spared not the angels that sinned, but cast them down to hell" (2 Pet. 2:4). Jesus said, "I beheld Satan as lightning fall from heaven" (Luke 10:18). Hell pulls down like gravity reaching up for a jet plane with a flameout in all engines. All kinds of down-wrong things originate there.

Jesus warns that hell is a place of "everlasting fire, prepared for the devil and his angels" (Matt. 25:41). The Bible talks a lot about hell, but it majors on how to stay out of there instead of how to get there. It reminds us of the mercy of God.

Heaven is up. Jesus ascended to His Father but said before going, "I go to prepare a place for you" (John 14:2). He even promised to come and get those who believe in Him. There's no comparison between His place and that other one—only contrast.

I heard about a couple of congressmen who were arguing heatedly. One told the other where to go. Looking up at the President, he said, "Mr. President, did you hear where he told me to go?" "Yes," said the President, "but you don't have to go."

Jesus suffered the hell of the cross so we wouldn't have to suffer the cross of hell.

Points on Prospecting

Abundance means more than enough. Some things come in that kind of supply—like life in Jesus. He said, "I am come that they might have life, and that they might have it more abundantly" (John 10:10). When you've got a plenty of something, it ought to be passed around. We are under orders to tell folks about our abundant-life Savior. The Bible calls it witnessing.

There are zealous folks around who have more zeal than tact. Fact is, their approach to a prospect may turn him more off than on. I heard of such a case.

My friend, Thurman George, told of being in a wreck. Got himself a real bad whiplash. In the hospital, he was in more than pain; he was in a right terrible position. The traction ropes and weights had his head so far back he had to view his surroundings through an overhead mirror. One thing sure, he had to keep looking up no matter what mood he was in.

Being about as free as a crook in a jail cell, he was a captive audience for a couple of witnessing ladies. One leaned over him, right down in his upturned countenance, and made inquiry of his spiritual status. "If you died tonight, where would you go?" That didn't set too well with a man who felt he was already being hanged.

I don't know his answer, but he told me what he wished he'd said: "To Hall-Wynne or Howerton-Bryan." (A couple of our local friendly undertakers.) It wasn't that he was unappreciative of the good lady's intentions. At the moment though, he was more concerned about living than dying. With due respect, her approach was a little like a 747 jet liner heading for a landing on a short runway.

Happily, my friend knows where he's going when the Lord says, "Come."

It's a fine thing that the Lord can use all sorts of efforts to get folks saved. A direct hit is better than not even trying. But passing out the Water of life doesn't have to be like a dam bursting.

Jesus had kind of a quiet talk with Nicodemus about how to be born again (John 3:1*ff*). It worked, too. Got himself a new beginning and took a stand for Jesus (John 7:50-51; 19:39).

If, as the song says, "It only takes a spark to get a fire going," why use a blowtorch?

Popping the Question

Jesus said, "Ye shall be witnesses unto me, . . . unto the uttermost part of the earth" (Acts 1:8). Some of His avowed followers take this as an optional choice; some take it as a privileged mandate. Mark Hopkins opts for the latter.

Mark felt a continuing tug in his six-year-old heart. He just knew God was speaking to him. The time came when he gave his life to Jesus, joined the church, and was baptized. His happiness was as contagious as a big smile. The fact that "Jesus loves the little children" was as real to him as his mama's love.

Now Mark is no graduate of Witnessing School, nor does he know how to use the Bible to show someone how to be saved. But his desire for everyone to be a Christian is as compelling as Billy Graham's. Without hesitation or embarrassment, it's not uncommon for him to pop the question, "Are you a Christian?" to just about anyone.

Sometimes a serious question can get a funny answer—unintentionally. Depends on what the inquirer's words mean to the inquiree. That's what happened.

Mark's concern for a little friend in his class was embedded in the question, "Are you a Christian?" To which the

little fellow, in all seriousness, said, "Naw, I'm a Baptist."
How this particular situation was resolved is unknown. I
have an idea that Mark assumed his friend was not a
Christian. Maybe he put him on his prayer list.

Our assumption is that no matter what denominational
garb we wear, underneath is a Christian. And that's the
intention of Jesus. Sometimes it's nothing but a shroud
covering the spiritually dead life of the wearer. It looks
pretty good but is going nowhere.

I've known some Baptists who resemble Christ about as
much as the Wicked Witch does Snow White. Wouldn't be
surprised if some other denominations couldn't scrounge
up a sizeble crowd who also fit the description.

'Course, now, the Lord is neither pleased with nor deceived by what we claim to be and are not. To the hypocrites He said, "Ye are like unto whited sepulchres, which
indeed appear beautiful outward, but are within full of
dead men's bones, and of all uncleanness" (Matt. 23:27).
A man may say he's a Christian, but the Lord knows for
sure.

Maybe we need more Marks to make us face life's su-
preme question. The label we wear is secondary; being
Christian is primary. The two ought to be synonymous.

Man can organize multidenominations. Only Jesus can
create Christians.

"Ye must be born again" (John 3:7).

Little Comfort

Poor old Job was in worse shape than a centipede with
a corn on each toe. He was suffering something terrible,

needing a bit of comforting. One of his "friends" tried his hand at it. Bildad the Shuhite (some say he's the shortest man in the Bible—Shoe-height) had an ignorantly pat answer for Job's pitiful predicament. Bildad was theologically sure that God was punishing Job for sin.

In his misery Job vocalized his desire to pass on. Brother Bildad picked up on the cue and advised the poor wretch to call upon the Almighty. Said he, "If thou wert pure and upright; surely now He would awake for thee, and make the habitation of thy righteousness prosperous" (Job 8:6).

Not only was Job covered with body sores, he now was supposed to feel guilty. Soul sores. But the Bible says even though he had lost everything, his children had died, and he was sick all over, "In all this Job sinned not, nor charged God foolishly" (Job 1:22). The comfort he got from blundering Bildad was about as soothing as the potsherd he used to scrape himself with (Job 2:8).

We've all had dealings with "Job's comforters." Sometimes well-meaning folks say things that miss the mark by two-and-a-half country miles. It'd be better if they'd just sit in the ashes with us and moan a little. But at least they try—which is worth something.

Three-year-old Daniel offered to help his mama through a bad time. Like Bildad, his success was somewhat limited. Mama was real sick. The pain was the make-you-cry variety. Daniel said, "Mama, do you want me to sing you a song so you'll feel better and won't cry?" That sounded real helpful, and she must've expected the little cherubic voice to burst out with "Jesus Loves Me," or something equal to it.

Now instead of a Jesus song, Daniel intoned, "Dracula is coming, Dracula is coming." Coming nothing! As far as mama was concerned, the creep was already there in her innards. That was about as comforting as eyeballing a spook in the graveyard.

All was not lost though. Mama had to stop crying long enough to laugh and maybe hug the little "shoeheight." I reckon he crawled a little deeper in her heart that day. She'll remember him for his honest attempt as a comforter.

The Bible says, "Comfort the feebleminded" (1 Thess. 5:14). Maybe at times it sounds like the comforting is coming from the feebleminded. I 'spect that's better than not caring at all.

God gives good marks to those who try.

The Tongue Tells

A mouth is a right handy thing—makes going to the table worthwhile and is gifted in making conversation. Only thing, sometimes the conversation is of the raunchy type. The Lord put our tongue behind a pair of lips and a set of teeth, but the thing gets loose and runs away anyhow.

The tongue is not independent. It reaches down in the heart and dredges up what's there. Then it dumps the contents on whoever listens. It can be polluting, and always advertises the talker's inner stuff. Jesus said so: "Out of the abundance of the heart the mouth speaketh" (Matt. 12:34). He said good things come out of a good heart and evil things come out of an evil one. So our talking invites others to have a look at the real us.

The face is gone from my memory, so I wouldn't recognize her again. That's fortunate, for the poor soul embarrassed herself. The incident lingers. The post office stamp machine refused to cooperate, "aggrafretting" the lady. Her tongue made a quick descent to the storage room of words and selected one. It wasn't the kind her little boy should've heard coming from his mama. It was real nasty.

Now that was bad enough, but how come I know about it? Well, there was a large sign standing between her and me as I stood at the counter. I wasn't hiding, but I was hidden. Stepping into view, she was apologetic and flustered. She knew I was a preacher, for evidently she had seen me around. "I didn't know you were there," said she. Sure she didn't, for most ladies don't want the preacher to know they can talk that way.

My ministerial ears had heard the word before. It wasn't the worst there is, but to my knowledge, I've never used it in a sermon. Wouldn't do. The little kid might get his mouth scrubbed with soap for using it. In fairness it'd be his turn to wash his mama's, and might serve as a filter for the next batch coming through.

All of which brings a truth to mind. Jesus forewarns us about our responsibility in our choice of words: "I say unto you, That every idle word that men shall speak, they shall give account thereof in the day of judgment" (Matt. 12:36). If a bad one pops into mind, it would be better to swallow it than blurt it out. Less damage.

All of us offend in word more than we should. There's a way to do better. The psalmist said, "The Lord gave the word" (Ps. 68:11). You can be sure a word He gives will pass muster.

The Lord is not concealed behind a sign, and He's not deaf.

Taken for a Ride

"He's out taking a man for a ride," sounds pleasant enough and could mean a thoughtful person wheeling someone around who seldom gets to ride. Not so in the case at hand.

Stopping in to see my car salesman friend, John Thompson, I asked where he was. The nice lady at the desk came up with that reply. A funny bell rang in my head. My laugh triggered one from her as the double meaning registered. I said, "I don't believe I'd say it that way." We decided "demonstration" was a better choice than "ride."

Some car salesmen have been known to take folks for a ride in more ways than one. Not so with John. He could well be called Honest John, for that he is. He'll tell you what he knows about a car even if he risks losing a sale. He must sleep well.

I've dealt with some "men-of-the-lot" who gave you a skittish feeling. Like they had "ridin'" in mind. To one such fellow I didn't identify myself as a reverend. We're thought to be naive, not too smart about such things as earthly chariots, and easily "took." One car caught my eye. Trying to impress me with its worthiness, he said, "A preacher owned that one." Well, Sir, he used the wrong bait. Being one, I knew the thing was nearing its last wheeze. Else why was it swapped? Probably would soon be in that big junkyard in the sky. I'm 'most sure I missed a "ride" that day.

Now Satan has been taking folks for a ride since man's beginning. Only thing, he's long on promises and short on delivering. It all began when Eve said "God hath said" and Satan rearranged the words to "Hath God said?" (Gen. 3:1,3). She got taken for a ride and the whole human race climbed in with her. What a salesman! And what dupes we are to believe a liar.

Of course God offers some real attractive rides that lead to where He promises. Like Elijah. The old prophet took a stand against sin and wouldn't budge. When God was through with him on earth, "There appeared a chariot of fire, and horses of fire, . . . and Elijah went up by a whirlwind into heaven" (2 Kings 2:11). What a ride! Home with God. In heaven. Up, up all the way.

Why ride with the devil when God offers the ride of life?—forever!

A Name and the Gate

Something happened at the exit of Duke Hospital's parking lot not too unlike another something awaiting the Christian.

Preachers traipse hospital corridors, peering in on the sick, with no little frequency. To pay each time the car is parked would tend to make us sicker than the folks we visit. Knowing this, the generous administrators give us free parking. That way sick folks may get more ministerial ministering than they would if the parson had to pay. It has something to do with economics.

However, we are required to sign the ticket that the bell-ringing gizmo pokes at us upon entering. Name, position, and church identify the bearer as eligible for no-cost cartending. 'Course, it's risky for the hospital. Some shady, soul-sick character could claim he had had a call from the Lord who wouldn't know the Lord if he saw Him. If that is true, the gyp percentage must be low enough for the hospital to take a chance on the real reverends.

A gate and a guard encourage visitors to ante up before leaving the parking lot. Several times I have handed my ticket to the same lady, manning the booth. Each time she would look at the name on it and maybe give me a corner-of-the-eye glance to see if I could possibly be a preacher. Giving me the benefit of the doubt, she would touch a button. Then the horizontal bar would rise to a karate-chop position, clearing the way for exit. So far, all was as routine as a nurse dispensing pills. Then something would set it apart. "There ya go," she'd say. Some ticket takers say nothing, others say, "Thank-you." "There ya go" was her unconventional way. And go I would.

Suddenly, I saw a parable of eternal truth.

The Bible tells of "the holy city, new Jerusalem, coming down from God out of heaven" and speaks of "the gates of it" (Rev. 21:2,25). It says, "There shall in no wise enter into it anything that defileth . . . but they which are written in the Lamb's book of life" (v. 27). Also, "They shall see his face; and his name shall be in their foreheads" (v. 4).

With the eyes of the soul, I see the time when I've gone as far as this life allows. There stands the gate, guarding heaven's entrance against the unrighteous. Whoever the celestial keeper of the gate might be, he looks at me and sees nothing that recommends me for entrance. He looks again. This time he sees the name "Jesus" stamped on my forehead. He checks heaven's roster and finds my name written there in the blood of the Lamb. Smiling, he opens the gate, and says, "There you go." And in I shall go, as he watches me join the company of the redeemed.

A bit fanciful? Maybe. But Jesus is our way to heaven.

He said, "No man cometh unto the Father, but by me" (John 14:6).

Join me, will you?

Holy Excitement

"Onward, Christian Soldiers" is a marching song for those enlisted in God's army. Onward and upward is our direction. You'd think with what is behind us and heaven before us there'd be a modicum of enthusiasm moving us along. It's not always the case.

Some of us are about as excitable as a former teacher at Wake Forest University. He wasn't easily flustered, was soft-spoken, and maintained his composure under most circumstances. However, according to the story, he really blew it one day.

The football game must've been a thriller. Lots of hootin' and hollerin'. The unflappable prof was there, quietly rooting for his team. Then it happened. Wake Forest was on about the two-yard line, threatening to score. Dignity to the wind, the doctor of letters lost all control. He just plain got beside himself. Standing up and leaning toward the field, he "shouted" with all the voice he could muster, "Move forward, young gentlemen!"

Now the story may be apocryphal, but we were some kind of glad to think our respected teacher had an "exciter" that could be set off.

Christians need to be calm most of the time. But not as calm as the Dead Sea. There's a difference in being at peace and being calm. Some things ought to get us stirred up like cream in a churn. Deliverance from the enemy is one. The Israelites at the Red Sea is a good example.

"Between the devil and the deep blue sea" is familiar territory, but Israel was between Pharaoh's army and the deep Red Sea. The Bible says, "They were sore afraid" (Ex. 14:10). Means they were real scared. "And the Lord said unto Moses, . . . speak unto the children of Israel, that they go forward" (v. 15).

You can feel the excitement as they went forward, with the Lord, on dry ground through the walls of water. Pharaoh's horde was drowned wholesale. The saved folks were so happy they "feared the Lord [stood in awe of Him], and believed the Lord" (v. 31). In the next chapter, they had a singspiration and started toward the Promised Land.

We found ourselves between the devil and the abyss of hell. Then we saw Jesus and the cross. It is said of Him: "Through death he might destroy him that had the power of death, that is, the devil; And deliver them who through fear of death were all their lifetime subject to bondage" (Heb. 2:14-15).

He says, "Come unto me" (Matt. 11:28). The enemy is defeated, we are free and moving forward toward our Land of Promise—heaven!

That's exciting!

2
Tall Truths from . . .
Using the Gift of Prayer

Rock Breaker and Razor Wrapper

Harold Kuhnle was my pastor when I was in those formative teenage years. During his stay at our church, I answered God's call to preach. His influence has been a lifelong choice blessing. One of his greatest contributions to my life is in the arena of prayer.

I've seen him on his knees with us young people; I've heard his voice lifted to God in earnest prayer. And God's answers came. He preached often on prayer, using effective illustrations that made praying more than a respectful duty.

I remember hearing him talk of difficult situations that need to be brought under continual prayer. He said it's like breaking a boulder. The sledghammer falls against it the first time and bounces off. No visible effect. Repeated blows follow. Still no evidence of anything happening. But then one final swing of the mighty hammer, and the rock breaks open.

Then questions would follow. Which blow of the hammer broke the rock? The first? The last? The answer: A combination of them all. Every strike was stored up inside the boulder; every one contributed to the final change.

Jesus said, "Men ought always to pray, and not to faint"

(Luke 18:1). Paul said, "Pray without ceasing" (1 Thess. 5:17). And James said, "The effectual fervent prayer of a righteous man availeth much" (Jas. 5:16). These are instructions on how to break "boulders." And the number of such hard-rock needs is not a few.

The other illustration has to do with how to handle folks equipped with cutting tongues. He said you can hold a double-edged razor blade between your fingers without getting cut—if the blade is wrapped up. Likewise, when finding ourselves in the presence of someone who is trying to cut us with words, wrap him up in silent prayer. Pray for him right then, and he will be unable to do any permanent hurt.

And while we're at it, we'd better double-wrap ourselves to keep from cutting back.

Amazing how it works.

Jesus said, "Love your enemies, bless them that curse you, . . . and pray for them which despitefully use you, and persecute you" (Matt. 5:44). He did, and does.

Harold Kuhnle was aware of the world being cluttered with "rocks" and "razors." He learned how to handle them and taught others the technique. He always walked close to the Savior who showed him how.

Maybe if more of us would rap the "rocks" *with* prayer and wrap the "razors" *in* prayer we'd be surprised at what the Lord would do.

Hit and Miss Praying

Sharing in a prayer meeting with Jesus, His disciples wanted to learn how real praying should be done. "Lord, teach us to pray" (Luke 11:1), they said. And He did. His prayer principles have been available for about twenty hundred years, but a lot of our praying leaves something to be desired. What passes for prayer may be about as close to the real thing as Venus is to Earth.

I heard of one preacher who remembered during the benediction an announcement he forgot to make. Not wanting to rile the ladies, he thought it best to get it in. He figured, no doubt, the Lord would understand and fix up a blessing for the occasion. So the crafty parson said, "And, Lord, bless the WMU as they meet at Mrs. Brown's home, Tuesday night at seven-thirty." That was helpful to the womenfolk, and the Lord wasn't apt to make any mistake as to what, when, and where the blessing was to be sent. I've heard of "dial-a-prayer," but that was a fine example of "announce-a-prayer."

A fellow-student at Wake Forest was reported to have addressed the Lord with a particular petition. The ol' boy was convinced prayer is effective, but he was so much in love he wasn't taking any chances on a misdirected answer. So, praying for his girl, he gave the Lord her post office box number. I doubt that the little doll lived there, but at least it gave a strong hint as to her whereabouts.

There's the story of the dedication ceremony of a railroad. To add dignity to the occasion, a renowned reverend was asked to lead in prayer. He had it all written out and read it. A real proper kind of prayer that echoed more head than heart. One observer remarked, "Well, I reckon that's the first time the Lord's even been writ to by the railroad."

Maybe all our praying should be more in the spirit of Dr. Hersey Davis who taught at Southern Seminary. He'd begin his class with a prayer, sometimes the hand-over mouth-mumbly-kind. After invoking heaven's blessings on the lesson and the learners, a student said, "Dr. Davis, we didn't hear you." To which the devout doctor replied, "I wasn't talking to you."

The Bible says, "We know not what we should pray for as we ought: but the Spirit itself maketh intercession for us with groanings which cannot be uttered" (Rom. 8:26). Glory be for extraterrestrial help! Our words may not always come out right, but God knows how to sort them out and send answers.

The throne of grace must get bombarded with a barrage of strange requests. They say there's a lot of joy in heaven. It's possible some of our prayers give the angels reason for smiling.

Puzzling Praying

"For the eyes of the Lord are over the righteous, and His ears are open unto their prayers" (1 Pet. 3:12). What a delightful truth that God looks at us and listens to us.

Now prayer is not always rightly understood by those around us who look and listen. A couple of examples give credence to the statement.

Preacher T. L. McSwain ordered a meal in a restaurant. The waitress set his plate in front of him; and, as his custom is, he bowed his head and offered thanks to the Lord. The blessing being concluded, he noticed the waitress still standing there, with her hands on her hips. Her caustic question matched her provoked expression. "Well, what's wrong with it?" The puzzled parson replied, "Nothing. Why?" Her answer revealed more about herself than she realized. She said, "You had your nose down in it smelling it like there was something wrong with it."

Thanking God for food in a restaurant is the exception rather than the rule. Alas, even for Christians. I reckon the lady was more accustomed to seeing eaters pig out like hogs that never look up to see where the blessing comes from.

If T. L. explained his "strange" actions, he may have enlightened a waitress who couldn't tell the difference between a bowed head and a sniffing nose. Who knows, maybe his example caused a weary waitress to look up to the Giver of "every good gift" (Jas. 1:17).

Six-year-old Valerie heard her Uncle Mark "saying grace." In it he said, "Bless this food to the nourishment of our bodies." That's a pretty standard expression that has ascended to the hearing of God times as numerous as the stars above. But that's not what the little one heard. She seriously inquired, "Where's the nurse in our bodies?" Even Dr. Marcus Welby of TV fame would be hard pressed to answer that one. Maybe there are meals that would make a nurse in our bodies welcome. But both prayer and question were sincere; and God disregards neither.

I'm sure there are events mingled with our prayers that bring a smile to the kind face of our loving Heavenly Father. It makes us glad that His understanding is of the infinite variety. He looks deep into the heart of the matter and says, "The prayer of the upright is his delight" (Prov. 15:8).

Potent Praying

Saying prayers is like reciting a piece, praying is like talking with a friend. We're more apt to do some serious praying when it's fastened to a need.

I hold a fine memory of Watson Bowers, long-time member and deacon of Bear Swamp Baptist Church. He taught me a lot in my younger days as his pastor. Example and words were his teaching tools. He loved the Lord and people, and wasn't bashful in telling it. It'd take weather not fit for man nor beast to keep him away from church. I've heard of times when he'd be about the only one to make it to the meeting house, but he knew Jesus would be waiting for him. His pilgrimage lasted over ninety years.

Now when Brother Watson prayed, you'd know he was talking with his Friend. He'd lay hold on the horns of the altar and bring the Lord up to date on prevailing conditions. Blessings were asked and directed toward those needing them.

Before I pastored Bear Swamp, Albert Simms was the shepherd. He had several churches in the circuit and would swap about in his preaching duties. Fifth Sundays were days off. On one such day, he and his wife attended Sunday School, without advance notice. Brother Watson first spotted them near the rear of the auditorium during the closing exercises of the whole assembled Sunday School.

Albert remembers the closing prayer vividly. "Now, Lord Jesus, we ask you to bless Brother Simms today. Anoint him from on high, give him Heaven's holy unction, and as he comes to break the Bread of life to us, may

he have the great and mighty power of the Holy Spirit."
A long pause of awkward silence punctuated the prayer.

"Then with unbroken calm and cadence of voice," says
Albert, "Brother Watson continued his prayer: 'No, Lord,
this is the fifth Sunday, and there won't be any preaching
today.' "

I feel sure the Lord appreciated the update and caught
the blessing just before He started it on its way. It was
crouched and ready for Bear Swamp's preaching Sunday.

The Lord "loveth him that followeth after righteousness" (Prov. 15:9). Mr. Watson qualified, and surely his
prayers were delightful to his Father in heaven. Some of
them may have caused a few smiles in the angel ranks, but
a bunch of blessings found their way to earth because he
prayed.

"The effectual fervent prayer of a righteous man
availeth much" (Jas. 5:16).

A Mop and a Prayer

"To every thing there is a season, and a time to every
purpose under the heaven. He hath made every thing
beautiful in his time" (Eccl. 3:1,11). Thus said Solomon the
Preacher.

Sometimes man's timing gets out of whack and a could-
be-beautiful thing gets hit with an ugly stick. Example:

The heavens had bawled their eyes out for a season.
Enough rain had pelted the earth to have made Noah
gather mama, the youngins, animals by the twozies, and
hightail it for the ark. Real soggy.

During this time a Christian couple had rented their

basement apartment to a professedly Spirit-filled gentleman. His salvation is not in question, but the application of his faith leaves something to be desired.

The abundant rain began running into the basement, heading for the kitchen. The upstairs landlord grabbed bucket and mop and "swabbed the deck" like a sailor in the Navy in which he had served. For three solid hours he mopped with back-breaking labor.

It's debatable whether the tenant was afraid of water or work. But his aloofness from the flood was expressed in his sitting in the living room, drowning himself in two hours of Bible reading, while said mopping was underway.

Maybe he came to where Jesus said, "And the rain descended and the floods came, . . . and beat upon that house" (Matt. 7:27). Suddenly, he appeared from his cloistered study. With genuine sympathy and undoubted concern, he offered help. Said he, "Mr. Doe, you have a real problem there. I'm going in the other room and hold you up in prayer." And he disappeared like a "hant" at daybreak.

Well, sir, "Mr. Doe" probably felt like poking the business end of the drenched mop into the mouth of praying "Mr. Dolittle," asking him how it tasted. But he didn't. He just kept mopping—exercising his right to fume just a little. You see, the Spirit really is in control of this godly mopper.

The man who preferred sitting on his bucket to filling one with the trespassing H_2O must've been kin to a certain priest and Levite. Jesus said they took a look at the robbed, disrobed, beat-up victim of thieves and "passed by on the other side" (Luke 10:29-37). The helping-hand Samaritan won the Lord's approval—and the man's whose life was saved.

A "mop-and-bucket" verse says, "Bear ye one another's

burdens, and so fulfil the law of Christ" (Gal. 6:2). Most likely that's the law of love.

There's a time to pray and there's a time to mop. Better still, why not pray and mop simultaneously?

Holdup and Held Up

Riding on the smoke-puffing, clickety-clacking train, my thoughts were filled with the usual apprehensions of a college freshman traveling a long way from home. God's call to preach was ringing as clear in my heart as a church bell. Under the Spirit's guidance a school had been chosen. A new adventure had begun.

Ignorance is no credit to the ministry, so book learning is essential in replacing emptiness with substance. I was soon to discover that all truth is not between book covers but is often hammered out on the anvil of experience. One of the nonacademic lessons I would learn is that God protects in times of danger.

Mars Hill College, nestled in the beautiful mountains of North Carolina, was my destination. My accumulated two hundred dollars had to be stretched across the whole year. Late in autumn, the remaining hundred nearly changed hands.

My pocket was my bank. The thought of bandits never crossed my mind. I was to find out that all who pass through a college campus are not students. Some are trespassers more interested in low living than in higher learning.

My room in Brown Dormitory was separated from the rest of the campus by a lonely road. Late one night I had to walk along that road alone. In the silvery light of the Carolina moon, I noticed four or five fellows standing in the roadside ditch just ahead. Thinking nothing of it, I gave a passing "hello." What I received in return was no friendly exchange of greetings.

One of the bunch stepped up on the road. With a gun in hand and his not-so-brave face covered with a handkerchief, he issued an order. "Put 'em up!" I wasn't too well educated yet, but I had a pretty good idea of what "'em" were. My heart nearly stopped, but, for some reason, my feet wouldn't. I kept walking, only to hear it again: "I said, put 'em up!" Seemed a little louder that time. My heart now in my throat, the throne of grace (Heb. 4:16) was silently but boldly approached.

Failing to halt, when encouraged to do so, may have convinced the bad guys I was either courageous or deaf. I was neither. Anyway, one of the others had a solution to their frustrations. His words, "Shoot him (with an epithet)," made my shoulder blades almost touch. Such cringing I had never felt before. Quietly, but earnestly, I said aloud, "O God."

Still walking, I was sure my college career was going to be short-lived with not even a posthumous degree by which to be remembered. I looked up at the moon and beyond, prayed, and hoped that heaven's gates would open to welcome my imminent arrival.

I did not understand at the time why they allowed me to keep walking. Although I was not shot, I was nearly scared to death. The Lord was watching over His own, and I was to learn more of the reason why.

My mother, a spiritually sensitive lady, lived four hundred miles away in Louisville, Kentucky. At the same hour the drama was unfolding in the hills, she was awakened. She "heard" the Lord saying, "Bud's in danger!"

Now wide awake, she quickly knelt by her bed and prayed for her boy. Not knowing what kind of danger, she simply prayed for God's protective care. And God heard.

All of this happened forty years ago. I do not understand all of the mysteries of prayer, but I believe my life was spared that night because of my mother's response to the Lord's warning. I have lived in the assurance that "He shall give his angels charge over thee, to keep thee in all thy ways. They shall bear thee up in their hands, lest thou dash thy foot against a stone" (Ps. 91:11-12). In my case, it must also have meant, "lest thou art threatened to be shot."

Mom is now with her trusted Lord. Somehow, I have a feeling that He still hears her prayer, "Lord, take care of my 'boy.' "

And, thank God, He does.

Keep Knocking

Importunity. That's a five-syllable Bible word describing an important ingredient in prayer. The story is in Luke 11. It's about a man who had company to come unexpectedly. His cupboard was bare. At midnight he aroused his neighbor to borrow bread. The neighbor didn't want to be troubled, but the nighttime visitor wouldn't give up. He got what he needed because of his shameless persistance. And that's the meaning of importunity.

My wife and I saw the word illustrated at the beach. Through the motel window, we saw a dad, mom, and their little bitty offspring beach strolling. The little one straggled behind, acting about as happy as if his toe had been crab bitten. He cared nothing about the beauty of the ocean or the sandy beach, he wanted to be carried. So he'd stop, scream awhile, and run to catch up. Then he'd do it all over again. Finally all three were out of our sight.

Presently they came back into view. Guess where the pint-size noisemaker was? Yep, astraddle his daddy's shoulders! He was ridin' high, taking it all in and as content as a kid with an all-day sucker. He had won!

It didn't take an Einstein to figure out what had happened. He had "importuned" his pa. He knew his dad had the power to lift him up and wouldn't give up until he got what he wanted.

Now Jesus isn't saying God is like the bedded-down neighbor who doesn't want to be bothered. He is saying that if people know how to give good things, "how much more shall your heavenly Father give . . . to them that ask him?" (Luke 11:13).

God is not a reluctant giver, but some prayers take awhile to get answers. Circumstances may make them ineligible for immediate results. Jesus is saying, "Don't give up." For every genuine need, within God's will, there is a supply. Not knowing when or how God's answer may come, we have the faith-building joy of continual asking, and trusting.

Jesus summed up the story and applied it to us by saying, "I say unto you, Ask [and keep on asking], and it shall be given you; seek [and keep on seeking], and ye shall find; knock [and keep on knocking], and it shall be opened unto you. For every one that asketh receiveth; and he that seeketh findeth; and to him that knocketh it shall be opened" (Luke 11:9-10).

Shame on us if we don't persist shamelessly in seeking God's supply for our needs.

3
Tall Truths from . . .
Being Like Jesus

Gold or Straw?

Piercing ears is a custom that goes way back. (But it has usually been the women who have worn them!) "Them little hang-ee-down pieces," as "Gunsmoke's" Festus would say, can be beautified or uglied with a choice of earrings. It's up to the wearer.

I knew a lady who had "holey" ears. Nothing unusual about that, but what she did with them was a tad different from usual. On Sundays she wore gold earrings. During the week she wore broom straws. It was her own business, but it created talk. It made folks wonder why she wore straw most of the time when she could've worn gold all the time.

In pondering this piercing story, a golden bit of truth rings in our ears.

Paul says Jesus Christ is the only foundation on which a Christian can build a noble life. The goal is Christlikeness. He cautions us to take heed how we build on that foundation. The building material is like gold or straw. Durable or perishable (1 Cor. 3:10-12).

Now, in all honesty, we have to admit that we are a mixture of good and bad. No Christian is all gold or all straw. The high aspirations of one moment can be followed by some right mean stuff the next.

For most of us straw seems to be more plentiful than gold and more easily found. If a man's not careful, the values in his life will be more like a whisk broom than like a twenty-dollar gold piece.

The Bible says the day of judgment will test a man's work (1 Cor. 3:13). The gold that has been laid on the foundation will endure the testing fire. All that's good, pure, and approved of God will last—and bring a reward.

Straw stands for the selfish, ignoble, worthless junk we've mingled into our lives. It will be reduced to ashes, causing us to suffer loss. Great gaping places will appear in the "temple of God," which we are (1 Cor. 3:16).

The "straw man's" work has about as much chance of standing as the little pig's straw house had when huffed and puffed against by the big bad wolf.

Jesus said, "I counsel thee to buy of me gold tried in the fire, that thou mayest be rich" (Rev. 3:18). In light of eternity, that makes sense.

Why put straw in our lives where gold is meant to be?

Seeing What's Not

Imagination is the ability to see things that don't really exist. To the imaginer they are real. Often what one sees in one's mind is later brought into being. Inventions are results of what a person thought could be.

Now there are some things that are confined to the imagination and could never take on substance. They may just be fanciful but not devoid of value. This was demonstrated in a school for exceptional children.

The students were to draw pictures illustrating some phase of Thanksgiving. One little girl's contribution was a large cooking pot over a fire. When asked what that had to do with Thanksgiving, she replied with knowledgeable dignity, "There's a turkey in that pot!" Even though the bird wasn't showing himself, she knew he was in there. And that qualified it as a Thanksgiving picture. The little one saw with imaginative eyes, was satisfied, and probably wondered why others couldn't see.

Jesus has imagination coupled with power to create what He sees. He looks at us two-legged messes running to and fro across the earth. But He has depth perception, knowing, with His help, the sin-marred image of God within us can be restored. He sees what ought to be, offering to make it so. Only the Lord would dare imagine a saint out of a clotty lump of human clay.

But He did and does. Simon could cuss like a sailor and was no refined gentleman. Jesus walked through his heart's door. Now look at him—"Saint" Peter! Levi, loved about as much as any tax collector of that day, is now loved as "Saint" Matthew. James and John were surnamed by Jesus, Boanerges—"The sons of thunder" (Mark 3:17). The thunder was conquered when Jesus gentled them. Men gave them their "Saint" degrees.

Jesus took a look at Zacchaeus, a man about as straight as a mountain road. He knew the crooked can be made straight. Going home with the short rascal, who had caused others to come out on the short end of the stick, the Lord saw in him what was hard to see. Zack ended up promising to give half of his ownings to poor folks and quadrupling in restoration the amount he had swiped.

According to the Word, that's evidence of salvation (Luke 19:1-10).

Fact is, there's right much "turkey" in all of us. Jesus came to empty us of the giblets of sin and fill us with Himself. That's really cause for thanksgiving. Someone might look at us and say, "There's Jesus in that man!" Imagine that!

Big Ben

This is the story of a man who, without trying, touches the heart. Prominent in Christian and educational circles, but about as puffed up as an uninflated balloon. He has no sense of self-importance, but is highly esteemed by those whose lives he has enriched.

Ben Fisher. Preacher, educator, denominational leader, Christian gentleman. Big Ben, you might call him. Big in frame, bigger in spiritual stature. He has cut a big swath for good through the field of life. A fine blending of intellect and humor. He makes you learn, and he makes you laugh.

His "take the lower seat" attitude was matter-of-factly revealed one day. He was to deliver the baccalaureate address at an important university. He said, "They're going to give me another degree." Sound bragging? But wait. The real Big Ben rang as true as Westminster's famed one when he added, "I don't need it; I'd rather have two dozen ears of sweet corn." Makes you want to say, "Aw, shucks."

Ben has a way of fitting in like a comfortable old shoe. In semiretirement in Murfreesboro, North Carolina, he frequented the gathering place of a group of older men whose life's work was mostly done. Knowing that you don't push yourself into such a circle, he waited for an invitation. It came.

A man was sitting there with one shoe tied, the other untied. Ben noticed. The next day a repeat. With genuine interest, Ben asked a reasonable question: "What's wrong with your foot?" "Nothing," was the reply; "Why?" "Well," said the big 'un, "I noticed you have one shoe tied and the other untied." The laid-back gentleman said, "Aw, don't pay any attention to that. I get up in the morning and I tie one shoe. Then, if I feel like it, along about ten o'clock I tie the other one." Ben said, "I knew I was in the right group."

How refreshing to be in the presence of someone who has the right to do some glorying but who has no desire to do so. He reminds us of Paul who had some "out-of-this-world" experiences but wouldn't talk much about them. He wanted Christ to get the glory, and he didn't want to get in the way. His fear was, "Lest any man should think of me above that which he seeth me to be, or that he heareth of me" (2 Cor. 12:6).

Big-hearted, big-souled Big Ben, the gentle giant, has helped us see what Jesus can do in the life of a person. In him reverence and harmless revelry have been like a towering mountain peak above the misty clouds that overhang life's valleys.

Ben Fisher—fisher of men.

Jewels in the Making

The word *jewel* is a beauty. It conjures up visions of something sought and obtained, precious, treasured, protected. Jewels we may never have; but, bless our souls, a jewel we can be. At least that's what the Jewel Maker says in His Word.

In the prophet Malachi's day, some folks that could've been "Real McCoy" jewels were paste. They professed to be of the religious sort but were about as genuine as a string of pearls that never saw an oyster. It grieved the Lord, like it always does.

God always has His remnant—those who are not cheap imitations. They are the ones of whom it is written, "They shall be mine, saith the Lord of hosts, in that day when I make up my jewels" (Mal. 3:17). Imagine that! Jewels of God.

I saw one of God's jewels in a nursing home. Margaret Couch had brain surgery years ago. Her days are spent in a wheelchair, her vocabulary is limited. A smile wreaths her face, and you get caught in her heart-emanating love. With the "why" questions answer locked in eternity, she pointed to her wheelchair and said, "I don't know why." Touching the indention in her head, she said, "I don't know why." And then, with a hand raised toward heaven and trusting joy etched on her face, she triumphantly added, "[But] believe on the Lord Jesus Christ" (Acts 16:31). A sparkling jewel.

Jewels are found in dirt and rock by someone who knows their value. They have to be lifted out, cut, shaped, and polished to become treasures. Jesus finds us in the dirt of sin, lifts us, and begins the lifetime task of perfecting us. Often the polishing wheel of trouble is used to transform a "diamond in the rough" into a gem that reflects the glory of God's light.

Some jewels are priceless. Money cannot buy them. Our salvation is like that. The price was paid by Jesus on the cross. "Ye were not redeemed with, . . . silver and gold, . . . But with the precious blood of Christ" (1 Pet. 1:18-19). And we are precious and priceless to Him.

Jewels are kept in safe places. God is as apt to lose His jewels as a jeweler is to put a three-carat diamond in a holey pocket. With Paul we can say, "He is able to keep that which I have committed unto him against that day" (2 Tim. 1:12).

Folks like us, God's jewels? That's incredible!

Pork and Purses?

"You can't make a silk purse out of a sow's ear." Whoever coined that bit of philosophy must've meant it's nigh impossible to make elegance out of ordinary. Of course, as apt as not, the pig considers her ordinary ears are elegant. The point of view depends on whether you're pig or people.

A brain-rattling variation of that famous saying was heard at a trustee's meeting. Discussing the fate of an old, historical, time-eroded house, some thought restoration and remodeling unwise. One man favoring demolition felt it impossible to make it into something usable. He said, "It would be like taking a dog and making a sow's purse out of it." I think he had the purse and sow in the back of his mind, but by the time the thought became vocal, it was as muddy as a mired sow.

Hardly believing what I heard, it gave me that "What'd he say?" sensation. Couldn't help wondering what a sow would do with a purse. The only likely candidate imaginable was Miss Piggy of Muppet fame. There's doubt, though, that she would want a "doggy bag." Might be accused of going to the dogs.

Now if the original gem of wisdom speaks of impossibilities, the jumbled version lifts it into the realm of utter impossibilities. And there are such. Like time won't run backwards, you can't grow younger, you can't unsay hurtful words or unshoot a man.

However, in soul matters, there's a hog-size difference. What looks impossible happens when Jesus shows up. Comparatively speaking, "natural" man is like a sow's ear, and "spiritual" man is like a silk purse. You'd think one couldn't become the other. But Jesus was all the time causing it to happen.

There was the time He found a "sow's ear" at the well of Samaria and sent a "silk purse" into town saying, "Come, see a man, which told me all things that ever I did: is not this the Christ?" (John 4:29). And a whole herd of folks hurried to Him, got transformed, and said, "Now we believe, . . . for we have heard Him ourselves, and know that this is indeed the Christ, the Saviour of the world" (v.42). Silk purses all over the place.

Who says sow's ears can't be turned into silk purses! Why, it's the only kind of stuff the Lord has to work with.

From pork to purses—that's the way of the Miracle Worker.

On Being Good

"I press toward the mark for the prize of the high calling of God in Christ Jesus" (Phil. 3:14). Anything less than Christlikeness was an inferior goal to Paul.

Sometimes a little child becomes the incarnation of scriptural truth.

Valerie, nearly five, spent a few days with us. Being good is important to her. She tries real hard and has a high degree of achievement. Being able to give a favorable conduct report to her mother is also of importance to her.

Just before leaving on the return trip, she put a question to her grandmother. In fact, one question led to three. "Grand-ma-ma, was I good?" Naturally the answer was "Yes, darlin', you've been good." But that didn't satisfy her. "How good was I?" That called for a comparison. Grand-ma-ma wanted to make good real good. "You were as good as gold."

Now, with an ounce of gold selling for several hundred dollars, that would make a grown-up feel his goodness was high quality. To a little child, another standard was needed.

Valerie's final question revealed the deep desire of her little heart: "Was I as good as Jesus?"

Suddenly, the ground seemed like holy ground. Here was a child, behavior conscious, who wanted to measure up to the highest standard there is. Even though no one does in this life, it's the right kind of reaching.

When the disciples wanted to know "Who is the greatest in the kingdom of heaven?" Jesus called a little child and set him in the midst of them (Matt. 18:1-2). I have a notion He smiled at him (or her) and hugged him as He picked him up. With sanctified imagination, I see the greathearted Savior smiling and hugging Valerie as He took notice of her that day. It must've pleased Him greatly.

Jesus spoke of our becoming like little children as requirement for entrance into His kingdom. He said, "Whosoever therefore shall humble himself as this little child, the same is greatest in the kingdom of heaven" (Matt. 18:4). Maybe it has something to do with loving Jesus, trusting Him, and wanting to be good.

Wouldn't it be a fine thing if all of us wanted to be as good as Jesus? This old earth would tremble with joy, for then upon her would be a multitude of folks walking about doing good.

"God anointed Jesus of Nazareth with the Holy Ghost and with power: who went about doing good" (Acts 10:38). He did good because He was good.

With Jesus in our hearts, so will we be good. It's part of that "high calling."

"The fruit of the Spirit is . . . goodness" (Gal. 5:22).

Watch Out for "Don't" Poles

The woodpeckers of Emerald Isle Beach created a problem. According to a newscaster, they took a liking to the power-line poles. Not as a perch but as dandy things to peck holes in. Nobody seemed to know why. Various solutions were tried to stop the foul rat-a-tat-tating. They even hung up some plastic owls. They didn't fool the live, busy, chisel-beaked birds, though. They probably saw through the disguise and said, "You *can't* give a hoot, and we *don't* give a hoot."

Killing or trapping woodpeckers is forbidden, so some kind of coating was applied to the poles. It turned out they seemed to like the coated ones better than the uncoated. Real mysterious—maybe it was like icing on the cake to their taste buds.

Seems to me the folks facing the problem had one choice: replace the peckable poles with unpeckable ones. There's just no way to change the nature of a woodpecker. You could break his beak off, and he'd still pine to peck. He'll be what he is until he has drilled his last hole.

Now man is a lot like Mr. Woodpecker, especially unregenerate man. He's the one who pecks holes in all the reasons why he ought to accept Christ. So he keeps on being his same old self. Seems to delight in doing destructive things. And when those things are coated with "don't," he likes them even better. He's a tough bird to figure out.

There's a big difference between man and a woodpecker. The Bible declares that man can change. "If any man be in Christ, he is a new creature: old things are passed away; behold, all things are become new" (2 Cor. 5:17). I reckon that means his likes and dislikes are different. He may fly up the wrong pole occasionally, but he won't stay there like he loves it. The good Lord puts a pining in his heart for what's right. The old "don't" poles are still around, but those "in Christ" fly with new wings.

To be honest, we Christians have to admit our fondness for "don'ts." We'd like for folks to think the old nature has been "cemeteryized," but the thing keeps resurrecting. We find ourselves flying around some mighty strange poles. Even 'fessing Christians sometimes create havoc.

One test of a Christian is how miserable he gets when he sins. Makes him want to "fly" to the cross and get redirected. He's aware of a growing desire to stop perching on forbidden poles.

Maybe the world would be more impressed if Christians looked more like high-soaring eagles than woodpeckers with their claws dug into poles they ought not to be up.

What's That in Your Bag?

"Abstain from all appearance of evil" (1 Thess. 5:22). A fine piece of advice for Christians, but not always accomplished. A person can be as innocent of wrongdoing as a sleeping baby yet be accused and convicted of being an evildoer by a factless observer.

My teetotaler wife has allergy problems. Tap water is taboo, spring water is required. That's what caused the stir.

Going into a family-type restaurant, the green bottle of aqua pura was nestled in a brown bag. Real suspicious looking. Amidst a few stares, we headed for a table. The manager must've had experience with brown-bagging rule breakers. Accosting her, she was firmly informed, "Lady, this is a nonalcoholic establishment." Her innocent look was convincing enough when she assured him it was nothing more than spring water. She remarked later, "I'm sure glad I didn't say branch water."

The spring water explanation was sprung on the little waitress, adding that "my husband is a Baptist preacher." She, too, seemed convinced, though on the surface you couldn't tell for sure about either.

Nearby eaters had that knowing look in their eyes. Seeing her down the stuff by the glassful was enough to make 'em bugeyed.

Now the disturbing thing about the "is it or is it not" episode is this: a few learned the truth; many jumped to their own conclusions—based on what they thought they saw. It's the sort of thing that cranks up the rumor mill.

A Christian should be as particular of his walk as a high-wire walker. A bad move not only disappoints the watchers but can damage the walker. He needs to say, "The Lord . . . will make me to walk upon mine high places" (Hab. 3:19). Walking with Him trims the margin of false accusations leveled at us.

There's another "warning" label on this sort of non-booze bottle: be a fact finder before being a finger point-er. Often we are as quick to assume the worst about folks as we are to defend our own innocence. Truth is, we just plain don't know what's in the other fellow's "brown bag."

Paul ties the two lessons of this abstinence yarn togeth-er eloquently by saying, "Let us not therefore judge one another any more: but judge this rather, that no man put a stumblingblock or an occasion to fall in his brother's way" (Rom. 14:13).

We'd better scrutinize the "bottles" and "bags" we tote through life—for Jesus' sake.

Like a Tree Transplanted

Hear the story of the little red maple tree.

Across the street, on a wooded lot, a red maple had sprouted and was growing. It was a spindly little thing, nestled among the tall pines and other tangled growth. Thin of trunk, supporting twiglike arms reaching heavenward, it measured maybe four or five feet. Bedecked in autumn leaves, it spoke in mute beauty of its rightful place in the scheme of God's creation.

But an ominous cloud hung over the lot. A "For Sale" sign prophesied that one day the lot would be cleared and all such worthless encumberances would be hauled away. Knowing this, there was a just-right spot in our backyard that seemed to beg for a pretty tree. So, with care and loving hands, the doomed tree was transplanted into a peat-mossed hole, watered, and is now safe to fulfill its destiny. From the curtained kitchen window, it will be like a growing picture in a frame.

Not many days after the little maple was saved, a chain saw began to roar and a bulldozer began to rumble. It would have stood no chance against such awsome power. Its place against the sky would never have been.

Having been moved from the devourer's way, the little tree could shout for joy. Poetically, Isaiah says, "All the trees of the field shall clap their hands" (Isa. 55:12). I've seen this one wave its little arms to the wind, like it's happy to be alive.

Now hear the story's application, that it might become a tree of life.

Man often finds himself living in the undergrowth of the world. He's entangled in things that can choke him to death. Satan, with "chain saw" and "bulldozer," is ready to move in. He has power to cut, devour, and destroy.

But Jesus, "Who his own self bare our sins in his own body on the tree" (1 Pet. 2:24), gently lifts us "out of the miry clay" (Ps. 40:2) and transplants us. That bit of heavenly horticulture depends on our disgust with ·destructiveness and our desire to be moved. It's called being saved.

Jesus places us in the soil and sunshine of God's love, enriches us with His own self, and waters us with streams of mercy. By the power of the Holy Spirit, we grow into trees of righteousness. A nurtured Christian becomes a thing of growing beauty in God's eternal kingdom.

"Those that be planted in the house of the Lord shall flourish in the courts of our God" (Ps. 92:13).

All praise to our great Transplanter!

4
Tall Truths from . . .
Shootin' Straight
on Money Matters

Scratch with Caution

It was foolish and dangerous. A mutt plopped down in a busy street, scratching his fleas. Being his own personal fleas, I reckon he figured he could scratch 'em wherever he pleased. Seems his judgment of a scratchin' place wasn't much to howl about.

Now maybe fleas, giving you a fit, would overshadow the possibility of getting flattened by traffic. You might say he was suffering from "flea-bite-us," which clouded his priorities of taking care of more important matters. Like survival.

The thumping of his hind leg against his flea-infested belly no doubt felt good. But he needed to say, "If I don't find somewhere else to scratch, I'll be dog gone!"

It's not exactly uncommon for folks to spend a lifetime scratching in the wrong place for relatively unimportant things.

Man, being body and soul, shows higher-than-dog-mentality by paying more attention to the forever than to the for now. Things, though necessary, don't amount to much if that's all we have when the reckoning day comes.

Jesus tells of a farmer with about as much forethought for the future as the itching pooch. His plentiful crops required bigger barns, so he figured on pulling down the old ones and building bigger ones. He aimed to say to his soul, "Soul, thou hast much goods laid up for many years; take thine ease, eat, drink, and be merry" (Luke 12:19). But crops don't make good soul food.

The poor soul made a belated discovery. When God said, "Thou fool, this night thy soul shall be required of thee" (v. 20), he heard the crashing of his intended earthly barns, and his hopes and dreams. That's what you call scratching for life's meaning in the wrong place.

Someone has said the soul is shaped like God, and He alone can fill that place. He does it through Jesus. "He that hath the Son hath life" (1 John 5:12). Scratch through all the short-range reasons for living and you come to Jesus— "The way, the truth, and the life" (John 14:6). He gives meaning and fulfillment to life for now and forever.

An earthbound, selfish life finally gets run over by time. All of the frantic scratching for stuff turns out to have about as much long-range value as a pile of dead fleas.

We'd better be particular about what we scratch for and where. The outcomes of our choices are different.

A Tip on Tithing

A story in one Sunday's bulletin gave birth to this story. It was about a man who gives 10 percent to the Lord's work and 15 percent for a tip at restaurants. A friend remarked that he must think more of the waitress' service than he does of God's.

Bobby Taylor read the story and asked his son, Troy, how much he put in the offering that morning. Troy, who fortunately has been taught to tithe, said, "I put in my tithe." Then Bobby asked him, "How much do you tip at a restaurant?" His answer, "Fifteen or twenty percent. Why?" Bobby said, "You must not have read your bulletin this morning." With an understandable note of alarm in his voice, Troy asked, "Have they gone up on the tithe?"

The tithe has been 10 percent from the days of Melchizedek (Gen. 14:18-20). Abraham gave him tithes of all out of gratitude. God has been receiving the tenth and blessing the givers ever since. Many go beyond the minimum and give offerings. Makes the joy bells ring. It's like giving your wife a present when it's not her birthday.

Troy is different from a couple I knew years ago. They had about as much conviction about tithing as an unconvicted sinner has about his sins. They made a yearly contribution to their church. I happened to visit them about the time they wanted to send their offering. The lady said to her husband, "How much do you want to thow in? I'm gonna thow in two-and-a-half. Do you want to thow in two-and-a-half?" That seemed to be a gracious plenty to him, so they each "thowed" in two-and-a-half. For five bucks, they got all the benefits of the church for a whole year. Didn't take the CPA angel long to record that gift.

God had something good in mind when He asked us to trust Him with 10 percent of what He sends our way. We can be as sure that there's a blessing wrapped up in it as that rain falls down instead of up. God's like that. He never harms those who love and trust Him. Banks pay dividends on our investments and God adds blessings to those who honor His Word.

The widow of Zarephath was about to starve. Through Elijah, she gave the last of her meal and oil to the Lord. And He gave to her by pouring meal from His barrel into her barrel and oil from His cruse into her cruse (1 Kings

17:8-16). She discovered that she could ride as safely in God's care as a baby kangaroo rides in his mama's pouch. So can we.

Under law, not to tithe was unlawful. Do you reckon that under grace it might be a mite disgraceful?

Old tithers never die; they just give themselves away.

A Stone Unturned

Every once in a while a spontaneous testimony turns out to be a heart-toucher and a mind-sticker. One was given in an evening church service that should've been heard by the whole church.

Betty Stone's billfold had been stolen. The thief did his thieving right in the church. (You have heard of a church mouse; this one was a rat.) The billfold was found on a Sunday morning and returned to her. Over one hundred dollars was as gone as yesterday. Betty was simultaneously glad and sad—glad for the find, sad for the loss. She went into the choir with a somewhat lifted spirit, but losing a hundred bucks is nothing to sing about. However, her faith in God is as unshakable as the Rock of Gibraltar.

Now hear the rest of the story. Her testimony went something like this. "I thought about not putting my tithe in the church the next Sunday. I could have used the money to help make up for what I had lost. Then I decided if I did that I wouldn't be any better than the one who stole my money." (She believes what God says in Mal. 3:8.)

"So I put my tithe in. By Wednesday, all of the stolen money had been replaced by friends who love me and wanted to help. The Lord took care of me."

You should have seen the joy on her pretty face and the smiles on the faces in the congregation. There was no boasting on her part, just glorifying the Lord. And His refreshing Spirit passed among us like the gentle rustling of angel wings.

The Bible says, "Whatsoever things are true, . . . honest, . . . just, pure, . . . lovely, . . . of good report; . . . think on these things" (Phil. 4:8). Betty did, acted accordingly; and God blessed. He always does. She also proved the promise —"My God shall supply all your need according to his riches in glory by Christ Jesus" (v. 19).

The word *stone* suggests something solid. This particular Stone gives credibility to the solidness of God's Word. . And God takes pleasure in honoring the faith of those who stand on His promises.

A testimony like we heard that night packs more punch than the preacher's prepared pronouncements. It's the kind that can make the nontither realize he doesn't have to be a pickpocket to be a pilferer in God's sight.

A Stingy Recollection

Out of my bag of memories, the occasional visits of Great-Uncle Morrison arise. He made some vivid impressions on his very young nephew. He had as much hair as a bowling ball but covered his shiny pate with a red wig during his waking hours. At night he tied his head up with a white cloth, knotted under the chin. He made quite a sight lying back in the old featherbed in the gas-lit bedroom. Shades of Ebenezer Scrooge! And a Scrooge he was.

He could squeeze a dollar until ol' George would turn blue. He was as tight as dried egg on a plate.

One day he was counting his money and dropped a penny. His eyesight was dim, so I found it for him. Holding it out to him, I childishly expected to get to keep it. Such gratitude I had never seen! His words are fresh today: "Thank-you, thank-you. I knew those little eyes could find it." And into the old snap-top leather pocketbook it went, to keep company with his much-loved coins.

Just think! For a penny I would remember him as a kind, generous uncle instead of Uncle "Scrooge" Morrison. He loved his money more than he did me. Poor soul, he left it all when he went.

Uncle Morrison is legion in the churches. They are those who love their money more than they love the Lord and His work. They even rob Him of His tithe and add it to their own stuff. But in the end, all is lost and the good that could have been done is left undone.

The Bible says, "God loveth a cheerful giver" (2 Cor 9:7). I reckon many of us could improve His opinion of us.

Straight Shootin' on Stewardship

Stewardship is a ticklish subject to preach about. Only thing though, those who haven't yet seen the light get a little twitchy instead of tickled. To those who have some grace growing to do, that fine Bible word *tithe* can be about as soothing as a dripping faucet.

A steward takes care of somebody else's property. Stewardship means you are a passenger in another person's ship. Contrary to popular opinion, God is the rightful owner of all things, and we are His overseers. The Bible says, "The earth is the Lord's, and the fulness thereof; the world and they that dwell therein" (Ps. 24:1). That sorta rankles our idea of things. We've been duped into thinking a title deed means ownership. "My" house, "my" farm, "my" car makes God a tenant, sharecropper, and hitchhiker. As humbling as it may seem, it's the other way around.

It takes a while for most folks to get a right understanding of what the Bible teaches about stewardship, and especially tithing. Leviticus 27:30 says it plain: "The tithe . . . is the Lord's: it is holy unto the Lord." For some, who need a dab more faith, it's kinda like trying to walk up a down escalator to believe it enough to become a tither.

Stewardship was my subject one night in revival. Unexpectedly, I got an assist that rattled me a bit. It came from the pastor, Harold Steen. He was hoping all of that mighty preaching would help some of his people believe it the way God says it. Having found the joy of tithing himself, he wanted them to find it, too.

Harold, being a hunter, often thinks in hunting terms. He's as straightforward in what he says as a rifle ball and about as inhibited as a rabbit in a carrot patch.

Either thinking I needed help or that I was on the verge of bagging some game, he interrupted. His deep, resonant voice boomed out, "Crate, keep shootin' in that same hole; they're in there." Well, Sir, after that, I don't recollect if I had any shot left. Felt like I'd been shot, but I kept on. If we got any converts that night, the Lord only knows. I 'spect the only part of the sermon that anybody remembers is the shot fired from the pew by the concerned parson. Who knows, maybe the Lord drew a few folks out of the holes of doubting His Word or of failing to claim His promises.

Relinquishing our ownership rights gives God room to pour out blessings. He says He will open heaven's windows and do just that (Mal. 3:10). Those who trust and obey find that the windows are not stuck.

We can send some earthly coin on ahead by investing in the Lord's work down here. It's called laying up some treasure in heaven. That being done, as the song says, "There's a gold mine in the sky."

It's just as sure as shootin'.

Tale of a Tot's Tears

Eight-year-old Arlinda Bowen was sitting on the front row in church between her mother Carolyn and grandmother Martha Rowland. She was crying as if her little heart were broken. It was offering receiving time, so accompanied by the offertory, I stepped down from the platform to find out what was wrong. She hadn't misbehaved, so her mama had neither pinched nor scolded her. Why, then, the tears?

My ol' heart was about to be as moved as a ninety-year-old sinner getting saved. She was crying because she didn't have any money to put in the offering plate! She knew that folks who love the Lord just naturally want to give Him something. And here she was, full in heart but empty in hand.

Now Martha, as tender of heart as a valentine verse, found a couple of extra quarters in her bag and gave them to Arlinda. Lovingly she placed them in the returning usher's plate to intermingle with the other love gifts. No need to cry anymore, for love's desire had been fulfilled.

Three things were accomplished that day. God received an offering of tears to put in His bottle—"Put thou my tears into thy bottle" (Ps. 56:8), fifty cents more was invested in the Lord's work, and a little child touched the heart of the congregation when the story was shared. Jesus said something about becoming as little children to enter the kingdom of heaven (Matt. 18:3). Arlinda showed us a little of what that means.

In all of my preaching years, I had never seen anybody cry over not having an offering to give. Some chilly-hearted folks may conjure up some inner tears when they give unwillingly, but not so among the hearts fired with the love of God.

Sometimes the preacher feels like bawling his eyes out. He preaches on the goodness of God toward good givers and is met with quizzical looks on the faces of doubting hearers. This must grieve the good Lord, too.

But then there are those who share God's concern for His people. Like Jeremiah, they lament, "Oh that my head were waters, and mine eyes a fountain of tears, that I might weep day and night! (Jer. 9:1).

That kind of crying leads to visionary giving that sees, not a lifeless, felt-bottomed offering plate, but a hand with a jagged scar in the palm like a nail hole.

The world could use more Arlindas.

Beat-Up Tither, Laid-Up Tithe

Howard Holley is a town official in Burgaw, North Carolina, and a respected leader in the Baptist church. His perfect Sunday School attendance is better than forty years. That's longer than the Israelites meandered in the wilderness. He, like they, has enjoyed many blessings from the Lord; but even Christians are not exempt from times of trouble.

Howard's skirmish with the forces of evil came like a bolt out of the blue. He was mugged by two thugs in a shopping mall rest room. They blacked and blued him without mercy, robbed him of about a hundred dollars, and fled like the cowards they are.

That kind of experience demands some explaining when you look like you've been in a brawl. And it takes a man of faith to see something in it for which to thank God.

Howard was "testifying" at church. His battered head gave credence to his story, but something he said stuck like glue in the minds of the unbattered listeners. He said, "They got my money, but they didn't get the Lord's. I had put the tithe aside and left it at home."

Now here's a man who could endure the loss of a hundred dollars, but who would've grieved deeply if the Lord's money had fallen into the hands of thieves. He encouraged the people to put God first.

I wouldn't be surprised if some folks didn't feel like they'd been punched in the heart. It's not uncommon for us to let God's work suffer loss instead of us. Like the little boy who was given two nickels. One was to put in church, the other for him to spend. He dropped one which rolled into the sewer. Sympathetically he said, "Well, God, there goes your nickel."

I guess Howard believes Proverbs 3:9-10: "Honour the Lord with thy substance, and with the firstfruits of all thine increase: So shall thy barns be filled with plenty, and thy presses shall burst out with new wine."

In spite of appearances, he still was filled with plenty of

God's blessings. His head may have felt like it would burst, but his lips burst forth with praise. For God was with him in a time of trouble, and the tithe, which "is holy unto the Lord" (Lev. 27:30), made it into the treasury of the Lord.

God's work is financed mostly by those loving-hearted folks who "Upon the first day of the week . . . lay by him in store, as God hath prospered him (1 Cor. 16:2). They'd sooner take a beating than let the devil beat them out of honoring the Lord.

Jesus always looks favorably on the Howard Holleys who grace His church.

Baptism and Pocketbooks

Some folks have funny (funny as in peculiar) ideas about giving to the church. A happening years ago at a creek baptizing illustrates.

A certain believer had a couple of sparsely furnished rooms in the upper story. He was smart enough to accept Christ as his Savior, but church finance was a little beyond his reach.

The day came for baptizing. He must have known that church membership includes giving, for when the preacher put him under and brought him up, he did a notable thing and impressed the onlookers, too. He reached into his soggy pocket and pulled out a quarter. Thrusting it toward the preacher, he said, "Here, take this. An' you ain't gonna get no more."

It's true that salvation is free. (Free, that is, to us but mighty costly to Jesus.) I suppose the saved and drenched brother figured everything else related to the church was free, too. At least it was not to cost over two bits.

Understanding sympathy is due someone with limited mental furnishings. But what about those with well-furnished upper-story rooms, who have never furnished their hearts with the words of Jesus, "Freely ye have received, freely give"? (Matt. 10:8).

The church can no more do its work without money than a steam engine can pull a heavy load without fuel. Most folks realize this and symbolically baptize their pocketbooks when the rest of their self is baptized.

I suppose you will always have free riders on the gospel train. Then there are cut-rate riders who make the journey and enjoy the accommodations because someone else subsidizes their ride.

The joyful riders are those who are so in love with Jesus and His church they pay full fare. The Bible calls it bringing the tithe into the storehouse (Mal. 3:10). The overflow is called an offering. "Bring an offering, and come into His courts" (Ps. 96:8). And God is reported as loving cheerful (hilarious) givers (2 Cor. 9:7). These are the choice souls who want to help a whole crowd of folks get aboard God's glory-bound train.

Baptism signifies a full commitment to Jesus. A baptized two-bit giver is all wet.

Trail of a Tither's Testimony

"Train up a child in the way he should go: and when he is old, he will not depart from it" (Prov. 22:6). That verse has been fulfilled in my being a dyed-in-the-wool tither.

By precept and example of my teachers, I learned to walk in the light of God's Word on tithing. It all began when I was but a child.

I cannot remember when my mother did not tithe. During the Great Depression, Dad's railroad wages were cut. For a while, four of us lived on forty dollars a month. Mom returned the Lord's tithe to Him. Robbing God was as unthinkable as robbing man.

We were never homeless, cold, hungry, or in want. Why, my sister and I even had a nickel to spend for small firecrackers one Fourth of July. I can still hear their puny little pops. I learned that God takes care of those who trust Him by acting on His Word. Times were tough, but God was tougher.

Stanley Reed, exampler of real Christianity, led our Junior Department in Sunday School. Junior boys forget a lot, but one thing I remember. Stanley was a tither, plus. To him, tithing was the minimum. He was a 20 percenter. Without boasting, he just did it. He was one of the happiest Christians I had ever known, loving the Lord with his heart and wallet. With indelible ink, he wrote a message on a young pilgrim's heart.

Our pastor, Harold Kuhnle, emphasized tithing in his preaching and practiced what he preached. He led our church to be a fifty-fifty church. One year, more was invested in missions than at home. Folks who tithed made it possible. And a teenager's commitment to tithe was more beautifully woven into the fabric of his life.

God's provisional care continued through college and seminary days.

The first year of college was begun with a little less than $200, the second with $180, the third with $153, and the fourth with $40. I guess it's a good thing I finished when

I did. Yet, at the end, I owed only $150. I worked, tithed, and God blessed.

Three seminary years were completed with a wife, a baby, and a small indebtedness on a car. It was a combination of faith and work, living in the care of a loving Heavenly Father. The Lord has always known how to multiply the loaves and fishes when they're given to Him.

Through all the years God has sent His supply for every need. Four children were reared, valleys of sickness have been trod, lean times have come. We have known the ups and downs common to humanity, but always there has been God. His commitment to care for His own is guaranteed for life.

Tithing does not buy God's favor. It's an act of loving obedience that enables Him to keep His promise—"I will . . . pour you out a blessing" (Mal. 3:10).

Fer or Agin

Sometimes a person's dreams are nearer right than his wide-awake reasonings. That seemed to be the case of a certain "aginer" church member. I heard the story years ago.

The church was considering adopting the budget plan for the first time. The proposal met with strong opposition by a man whose middle name should have been "Against." He was hooked on the old ways and about as progress minded as a balking mule.

His adamant stand was voiced thusly: "Preacher, I'm agin that burjit. We ain't never had no burjit, we don't need no burjit, and I'm agin the church having a burjit."

That was designed to put the preacher in his place and to settle the matter.

God has His ways of dealing with those who stand in the way. Like Nebuchadnezzar, the closed-minded brother had a dream. Not understanding its meaning, he told it to the preacher.

"Preacher, I dreamed the other night we wuz votin' on that burjit, and I was fer it. What'dya reckon that means?"

The preacher must've been a descendant of Daniel who was given wisdom to answer ol' Nebuc. He said, "I don't know. But one thing for sure: you've got more sense when you're asleep than you have when you're awake."

Daniel was rewarded for his dream interpreting. The record says, "Then the king made Daniel a great man, and gave him many great gifts" (Dan. 2:48). I have my doubts that the bold parson fared so well. Most likely he reflected on the whole matter from his next pastorate.

A person ought to have more sense about church affairs when he's awake than when he's sawing logs. Alas, many folks, awake enough to get saved, are dead-to-the-world asleep when it comes to financing the Lord's work. They need to hear this: "Awake thou that sleepest, and arise from the dead, and Christ shall give thee light"! (Eph. 5:14).

The Covenant Keeper

Benny Littlejohn served for a while as pastor in Puerto Rico. During that time, a story of premium-type commitment to the Lord was discovered.

A Puerto Rican church member earned between $200

and $230 per week. Not much for a man with a wife and four children in a high-cost-of-living country. Yet his giving through the church reflected his cost of loving. Better than $45 each week.

Now what in the world would cause a man to invest such a percentage of his income in God's work? By most standards, that's excessive, unreasonable, and unnecessary. Must be nobody told him there's no need to overdo a thing. Surely God doesn't expect that kind of fanaticism.

The preacher's curiosity needed satisfying. Admittedly, this brother's stewardship outstrips the average Christian's like a banker's life-style does a beggar's. So the preacher asked him why and how he gave so much out of his earnings.

He said, "Years ago, I made a covenant with God. I promised Him that each week I would give Him a little more than the week before—a penny, two pennies, a nickel, a dime. I have kept my covenant. It has taken thirty-five years to give what I now give."

The man made a vow. Wow, what a vow! He must have read Ecclesiastes 5:4—"When thou vowest a vow unto God, defer not to pay it; for He hath no pleasure in fools: pay that which thou hast vowed." God had Himself a wise man, not a fool.

Mr. Great Heart's answer revealed a pretty good understanding of conversion. He knew, that, along with the soul's salvation, such mundane stuff as money is included. Honest piety and the pocketbook go to church hand in hand.

This man's life speaks of a great love for God, the church, and her mission of introducing folks to Jesus. It speaks of obedience, trust, and faithfulness. It speaks of an investment in heavenly things that is beyond earth's calculating ability. It speaks of a day when "the saints are gathered home," and of having a part in making their gathering possible.

Who can know how many beautiful blessings God has sent upon him, like the refreshing dew? Or how He has supplied his every need? Maybe the joy of knowing he has kept his promise is enough.

The story of the covenant keeper tugs at the heart—perhaps igniting inspiration.

Without a doubt, God honors those who honor Him.

Payday—Prayday

Tithing can be a duty, a habit, or an act of worship. Only the latter expresses the attitude of the soul in the presence of God.

In the early 1960s, Harriett and I were Spirit-impressed to elevate our mode of giving. We were practicing tithers, knowing God said it is His plan (Mal. 3:10). For man to think he's smarter than God and has a better plan is like a first grader trying to teach the teacher. So the tithing question had long since been answered with a faith-born *yes.*

But there's giving and there's giving. A conviction began rising in our hearts like a beautiful sunrise. God was saying, "Pray each payday over the money I lend you." So we began. With regularity, paydays became times of receiving from the Father's hand and relinquishing ownership to Him. With thanksgiving, to Him the tithe was joyfully dedicated; His blessings were asked for the remaining portion's use. It became a lifetime practice.

What were the results, immediate and long range?

First—immediate. The devil was about as pleased with that decision as he is with one of his imps sassing him. He threw us a tote sack full of tricks.

No sooner had we begun honoring the Lord on this deeper level until three family members were in hospitals. Within six months, medical bills topped a thousand dollars, and not a dime's worth of insurance. In that day's economy, a thousand bucks would bulge your eyeballs.

Thinking he had won, the "Prince of Darkness" snickered, "You started praying over your money; now look at what's happened to you." He knew we were deeper in debt than ever. Being less than bright, he didn't reckon on "The Bright and Morning Star" (Jesus).

The Bible says, "Blessed be the Lord, who daily loadeth us with benefits" (Ps. 68:19). So we remained faithful to the commitment, believing "God shall supply all your need according to his riches in glory by Christ Jesus" (Phil. 4:19). He did.

In a short while the debts were paid, the test was passed. God was faithful. We had passed on to higher ground.

Then—long range. Never have we since been in a financial bind like we had known before. Four children received college educations. Victuals, dwellings, clothes—more than adequate. Blessings, earthly and heavenly—as uncountable as the multi-facets of God's abounding grace. Joy unspeakable—parented by obedience to our Father's will. And there's always something extra to give.

We have learned that "God is able to make all grace abound toward you; that ye, always having all sufficiency in all things, may abound to every good work" (2 Cor. 9:8).

"That thou givest them they gather: thou openest thine hand, they are filled with good" (Ps. 104:28).

Make payday a *prayday* and see what God will do.

Fresh Wind for Stewardship Sails

Gattis Perry had a student pastorate while at Wake Forest. En route to the church one Sunday morning, his wife asked him what was he going to preach. Tithing was his subject.

The young preacher had his message planned. "Abraham commenced it, Jacob continued it, Moses codified it, Nehemiah restored it, Malachi commanded it, Jesus taught it, Paul explained it, and the church needs it." I suppose he was ready to "let 'em have it."

Wives have a way of letting the wind out of husbands' sails. Carl Joy did it with one fell swoop. After a time of deafening silence, she said, "When are we going to start?" Now how in the world could a nontithing preacher preach on tithing with a thought like that banging around in his head?

A decision was in the making at about 9:30 AM on a highway that would lead to higher ground.

"How much money do you have?" she asked. "Two cents," he answered. "How much do you have?" he continued. "Ten dollars," she revealed. That was a tithe of what both had earned the week before so in their hearts they gave the ten to God and then gave it to Him through the church. I have a notion that Gattis preached that morning without feeling like a hypocrite.

On the way home, Carl Joy wanted a coke. Telling her that God was all out of cokes, he went into a drugstore, laid his two pennies on the counter and asked for two cups of water. The kind-hearted clerk gave him the water and returned the two lowly pennies. (What does the Bible say about a cup of cold water?)

The near-broke reverend had two cents, enough gas to get back to school, and no grocery money until the next payday.

One more stop was made to visit a church family. As they were going back down the driveway, the man ran out, waved his arms, and called them back. He said, "Preacher, about 9:30 this morning, the Lord laid it on my heart to give you this." And he stuck a twenty-dollar bill in Gattis's shirt pocket.

Telling the story about thirty years later, the grateful preacher said two things worthy of note. First, "We have never stopped tithing from that day." And second, "I'm not saying that every time you give God five dollars He will give you ten. But, if He doesn't, He will give you something better."

Obedience to God assures His care for us. Like the widow of Zaraphath, when she gave her last bit of food to Elijah, God's promise was kept. The record says, "And the barrel of meal wasted not, neither did the cruse of oil fail, according to the word of the Lord" (1 Kings 17:16).

The Lord is still in the "meal and oil" business to those who obediently trust Him, and He has no plans for bankruptcy.

5

Tall Truths from . . .
Using the Promises of God
in the Dark Places

Storm-proof Shelter

Storms. They come. Sometimes with more threat than performance. Sometimes with wild fury. Suddenly or with advance notice. But they come.

All through the Atlantic Beach night, the heavens had a heavyweight fight. Black clouds furnished the background for the jagged lightning, ripping its way across the sky. Cannon-like thunder exploded, followed by giant kettledrum-like rolls. Abundant rain, accelerated by the wind, pelted the windowpanes and did a war dance on the rooftop.

A storm creates anxiety. The lights go off. You wonder if the lightning will strike. In it all, you remember God's promise to be with you. But you're glad someone is there with you that you can touch. You pray.

Presently the flashes get less flashy. The thunder sounds more like an old tired, growling lion heading back to his den. And you know the storm has about spent itself. It didn't come to stay. Having belted you around for a time, it returns to wherever storms hide. And you remember there are more calms than storms. There have to be for us to endure.

There are similarities between nature's storms and the

personal ones we face. In their midst, God's Word comes like a mother's sheltering arms around her frightened child. "They cry unto the Lord in their trouble, and He bringeth them out of their distresses. He maketh the storm a calm, so that the waves thereof are still" (Ps. 107:28-29).

Like trusting God through a dark and stormy night, we learn to trust Him in soul tempests. Those that break within us; those caused by others that break around us.

Some temptation, with power like swirling water to pull us under, darkens our soul. The warmth of God's love clashes with the cold front of evil's reasoning. A storm rages within. And God says, "There shall be . . . a place of refuge, and for a covert from storm and from rain" (Isa. 4:6). Safe in there, the storm passes.

Some overwhelming sense of failure or disappointment or some disturbing fear can give a sinking-in-the-storm feeling. We cry out, "Master, carest thou not that we perish?" And, like He did on the stormy Galilean sea, He says, "Peace, be still!" Then to us, "Why are ye so fearful? how is it that ye have no faith?" (Mark 4:38-40). We find that the "winds" and the "waves" that storm the citadel of our hearts are still subject to His power.

"When thou liest down, thou shalt not be afraid: yea, thou shalt lie down, and thy sleep shall be sweet" (Prov. 3:24).

God is our refuge—especially in storms.

Three Thoughts About Trouble

Have you ever felt like your world was slipping out from under you? Then walk with me in the ocean's edge.

The water was about ankle-to-calf deep around my legs. Like wet tongues, the waves would lap the beach, then withdraw. Walking and looking down at the rippling water running at an angle over the corrugated sand made me dizzy. I felt about as steady as a sauced sailor. The shifting sand under my feet added considerably to my queasiness. But looking skyward negated the effects of the happenings around my feet.

Several thoughts sloshed around in my mind. They have to do with our troubles.

Thought 1: *The ocean, like trouble, can reach only so far. There are boundaries beyond which it cannot go. Even in storms the land says, "Hold on there, Mr. Raging Sea, this is your limit!"*

Trouble is as common to man as scales are to a fish. Job said, "Man is born unto trouble, as the sparks fly upward" (5:7). But he found God had limited what Satan could do. After passing through devastation, the same Job said, "I have heard of thee by the hearing of the ear: but now mine eye seeth thee" (42:5). God had said to the trusting man's troubles, "That's enough!"

Thought 2: *Like the moving sand, our foundations sometime begin to quiver, and makes us about as uneasy as being in a dinghy in a tidal wave. But when we feel the "sand" shifting beneath us, it's look-up time. Looking down is like getting caught in the undertow. Looking up to Jesus shifts our attention from problems to solutions.*

The psalmist said, "All thy waves and thy billows are gone over me" (42:7). Sounds like he was about to drown in a sea of trouble. But later he said, "I will lift up mine eyes . . . from whence cometh my help. My help cometh from the Lord!" (121:1-2). It works.

Thought 3: *Just beneath the surface of the mobile sand was a solid foundation. I found out you can wobble without sinking. Likewise, underneath our "sinking sand" is a foundation as solid as God. "They that know thy name will put their trust in thee: for thou, Lord, has not forsaken them that seek thee" (Ps. 9:10). We can sing, "From sinking sand he lifted me." God is as apt to abandon His trusting children as the ocean is to run dry.*

Jesus said, "Lo, I am with you alway" (Matt. 28:20). That's "low" enough for Him to walk with us through threatening waves.

Christians are unsinkable!

Nighttime Stories

Concerning the days of creation, the Bible says: "The earth was without form, and void; and darkness was upon the face of the deep" (Gen. 1:2). Then God created light, dividing darkness and light. He didn't do away with darkness, but fixed it so we wouldn't have to always live in it.

Darkness has its benefits. In it we sleep, see the star-spangled sky, the earth rests from scorching heat, and the nightingale sings. Of course there are some unmentionable things that happen under the cover of darkness, but God meant night for good.

I heard the story of a courting couple, traveling by train. Suddenly, they were in a tunnel. In the darkness, the young fellow did what comes naturally—he kissed his girl.

She got "bussed" on the train. All of a sudden the train emerged into the light. Caught embracing, he was embarrassed and knew he needed to say something. His subject-changing remark was, "You know, they say that tunnel cost $500,000." With her lips still tingling, the freshly kissed lass said, "Yes, and it was worth every penny of it."

Going through the dark makes you grateful for the light. Between Louisville and London, Kentucky, there are several railroad tunnels. Standing on the platform of the last car (coach not box), I rode through one. The old steam engine was belching smoke and spitting cinders, the clatter of the wheels was magnified, it was eerie dark and wasn't the cleanest place I'd ever been or the best smelling. But tunnels don't last forever.

Soon it was daylight again. What beauty the mountains, the sky and even the tunnel's exit! Without temporary times of darkness, we wouldn't know how to appreciate the light.

Beauty is often perfected in the dark. When I was a little kid, we had a cactus plant called night-blooming cereus. The large, fragrant, white flowers open only at night. I remember the times we would go out in the backyard to watch the blooms unfold and to admire the beauty revealed in the nighttime.

Most folks are acquainted with darkness of the soul. And that's the worst kind. At the time, those tunnels seem endless. But God gives us "tunnel vision" with which to see Him in the dark. Time comes when we emerge, sensing that a worthwhile something happened to us "in there." Day looks brighter than we ever noticed before. And the flower of faith blooms with new beauty.

From a patch of darkness, the psalmist said: "My soul waiteth for the Lord more than they that watch for the morning: I say, more than they that watch for the morning" (Ps. 130:6). He knew daylight was coming.

"The Lord is my light and my salvation" (Ps. 27:1).

Dumping the Dumps

Profound pronouncements pop up in peculiar places. Most residents in nursing homes are elderly, with problems of one sort or another. When the body aches, the spirit can get a little draggy, too. This condition was verbalized in a mind-catching way.

A lady, confined mostly to a wheelchair, frequently rolls herself into her friend's room. They enjoy "fellowship in suffering," which can be mutually beneficial. But sometimes the visits are shortened to advantage. Explaining why, my friend said, "When I'm down in the dumps and she's down in the dumps, I leave. It's not good to have two dumps in the same room." I guess you could say one of the dumps rolls away.

Nobody escapes trips to the "dumps." We all know their locations. The word *down* is accurate, for there's no path that leads "up" to the dumps. Fact is, the dumps are about as high as a dachshund's stomach is from the ground. It's as easy to get there as falling into a hole and as hard to get out of as trying to lift both ends of a heavy log alone.

When "two dumps" get together, down gets downer and the spirit of both sags like an overloaded clothesline. A clothesline can't stand but so much wet wash to be hung on it. Neither can people. Listening to too many soggy stories gives us that washed-out feeling.

You'd think those Bible folks were antidump. 'Taint so.

Some of them got so low they had to reach up to touch bottom.

Jezebel vowed to end Elijah's days of prophesying. She scared him so badly he ran like a scalded tomcat. Under the juniper tree, he begged God to take away his life. (Jezebel had already volunteered to oblige him in that way.) Forty days later he crawled into a cave and complained something fierce.

Both times God came to him. An angel joined him under the juniper and served him vittles, plus some encouraging words; and God called him out of the cave, speaking to him in a "still small voice." The Lord lifted him out of the dumps, and the revived prophet did a right fine piece of prophesying until he was caught up in a chariot into heaven. He was really up then! (1 Kings 19: 1-19; 2 Kings 2:11).

The great King David went to the dumps real often. For our sakes, it's good that he did. His accounts of getting out of them ring authentically. Once he said, "O my God, my soul is cast down within me" (Ps. 42:6). But then, "Why art thou cast down, O my soul? and why art thou disquieted within me?" His answer for deliverance was: "Hope thou in God: for I shall yet praise him, who is the health of my countenance, and my God" (v. 11).

Excursions to the dumps are part of the human condition; but a dump is a blighted area, and no one wants to live there.

It's best to dump our dumps at the foot of the cross. The Lord knows what to do with them.

Don't Be a Caveman

Cudjo's Cave is in the Cumberland Mountains near the place where Tennessee, Kentucky, and Virginia converge. At one point you have the unusual experience of standing in three states at the same time. There are even more unusual experiences in the cave.

Running under two states, the cave is deep in the heart of the earth. Above it are mountains of rock, dirt, and trees, reaching up twenty-five hundred feet. Inside are stalactite formations, great stone draperies, and calcite crystals. Dangerous drop-offs, pools of water, low overhead places, and slippery spots make you walk with caution. The trip through is awesome and impressive as long as the lights are on.

The eeriest part is when the lights are turned off. The darkness is as thick and black as the inside of a blackberry pie. The Bible speaks of gross darkness. One preacher said gross sin is 144 times worse than ordinary sin. Cudjo's Cave's darkness is 144 times darker than ordinary darkness.

Thoughts of being forever lost in there scare you out of your wits. You stand there immobile, unable to see the path, without any idea of where the door to outside is. The invisible people around you are equally helpless. Ol' panic is about to grab hold and give you a shake.

Then the lights go on. Darkness vamooses. You feel like blind Bartimaeus when Jesus gave him his sight. Following the guide, you see the door ahead. Beyond is the great outdoors. Once there you are engulfed in pure sunlight, fresh air, a new awareness of beauty, and thankfulness!

The incredible journey has its parallel in man's salvation experience.

The Bible speaks of "him who hath called you out of darkness into his marvelous light" (1 Pet. 2:9). Sin's smothering darkness makes Cudjo's lightless cave seem like high noon.

There being no superfluous words in Scripture, when it says marvelous light, it means marvelous. It's astonishing light, "a light from heaven, above the brightness of the sun" (Acts 26:13). Any person, led out of inner darkness, will marvel forever at the marvelous light Christ has given.

Jesus refused to condemn the world in its darkness but came to offer it light. He said, "I am come a light into the world, that whosoever believeth on me should not abide in darkness" (John 12:46). That's salvation!

A man would have to be a double first cousin to a mole to prefer a hole in the ground to the world above.

Locks Are for Lifting

The illustration was heard years ago, but the source evades me. Then I saw the real thing happen. It became "my" story.

On the edge of Louisville, Kentucky, a canal runs between a high and low level of the Ohio river. It contains a set of locks through which ships pass.

I watched a ship enter the first set of locks. The giant front gates were closed. Then the rear gates closed, making the ship immobile. Nothing seemed to be happening. But underneath, the intake valves were opened, allowing the water to flood the chamber. Gradually the ship was raised to the next water level. Then the gates opened, and the "lifted" ship moved into the next set of locks. The process was repeated until the ship was enabled to travel on the upper level of the Ohio. By means of the locks, the vessel went from low to high.

This is a parable of life. There are times when we are locked in. It may be sickness, disappointment, failure, or trouble wearing one of its many garbs. Being unable to move either forward or backward, we are forced to wait.

But something is happening without our knowing it. God has opened the valve of His love beneath us. His mighty power is at work. He's lifting us! We learn to "Rest in the Lord, and wait patiently for him" (Ps. 37:7).

Presently, the gates open, and we move out on a higher level. We discover our confidence in God to work all things for our good (Rom. 8:28) has risen to a new high. Depending on the complexity of our problem, the process may have to be repeated several times. Each time we rise a little higher. In the midst of it all, the Spirit whispers to our hearts, "The eternal God is thy refuge, and underneath are the everlasting arms" (Deut. 33:27). In God's arms our low level is limited, and we find His arms are strong to lift.

In those hemmed-in times we hear God say, "Be still, and know that I am God" (Ps. 46:10). There we learn to trust Him and dare to believe our troubles do not come to stay, they come to pass.

Ships are meant for sailing, not for staying locked in locks. Though temporarily necessary, locks are for lifting. Likewise, man is meant for the high places in God's plan. We go through the "locks," but we won't be left there.

God says, "Because he has set his love upon me, therefore will I deliver him: I will set him on high, because he has known my name" (Ps. 91:14).

Life is a series of locks. And the last ones through which we pass will find us docking at the port of heaven.

Sail on, my brother, sail on!

Wind Chimes

Al Austin is a craftsman of wind chimes. Hanging at the end of the carport, they add a dimension of beauty and pleasure—appealing to the eye and ear. If allowed, they also touch the heart.

When the weather is tranquil, no sound is heard. But you know the chimes are there. A breeze sets the heart-shaped pendulum in motion, and the disc-shaped clapper goes to work on the variable length pipes. Tunes of infinite variety go a-wafting.

Breezes of the zephyr sort produce gentle sounds. As the wind gets more courageous, the chimes respond accordingly. And when a storm passes by, they crescendo. The strength of their voice depends on the velocity of the wind. A composer would be hard pressed to write the songs they play, for they hardly ever play the same tune.

In the dark of a restless night, when sleep takes wings, how pleasant to the soul to be assured that your friendly chimes are awake, too. Their lovely tones become like chapel bells. Somehow the dark is less dark and loneliness is less lonely.

It's a parable of life-size proportion. Let the wind represent life and the wind chimes the presence of the Lord.

Sometimes the wind hardly stirs—times of peace. And God seems silent. But with the eyes of the heart you see Him there, and are glad.

Ill winds begin to blow, bringing trouble but not big trouble. He answers just loudly enough to give assurance of His presence. The ears of the heart hear Jesus saying, "Be of good cheer, it is I; be not afraid" (Matt. 14:27). And fear that was arousing lies down at the sound of "heaven's wind chimes."

Then a real nor'easter hits you. Jagged lightning splits your sky, and angry-voiced thunder pitches a fit. Major league trouble has swooped down upon you. But the Lord, like the wind chimes, fairly yell, "I'm here! I'm here!" No fury can still His voice; for the stronger the wind, the clearer He calls.

The believing heart says, "Behold, God is my salvation; I will trust and not be afraid: for the Lord Jehovah is my strength and my song: he also is become my salvation" (Isa. 12:2).

As wind chimes are to the wind, so Jesus is to those who trust in Him, and listen. His repertoire of soul music is inexhaustable, and His combination of notes are as different as the needs. Let the winds blow, for the sound of His reassuring voice is heard in little troubles, big troubles, and in times of no trouble.

Eyeballing Fears

Standing near the hospital elevators was a lady-in-waiting. "Are you going down?" she asked. I was, but hopefully not too far down. Identifying herself as an evangelist, she confessed her fear of riding an elevator alone. No doubt, she knew the Lord was with her. Still, somebody she could see would give assurance. Two could holler louder than one in case the doors and the floor didn't line up.

At first thought, it seemed contradictory that a lady preacher would fear such a contraption. "Going up" was her natural inclination, but maybe the thought of "going down" tore her up. Whatever triggered her fear was none of my business. She was a damsel in distress, and I got to ride shotgun and felt heroic.

Then I remembered. Time was when a rickety old hoist held me in fear. I had the humbling but dubious honor of being garbage man for Manly Hall at seminary. Found out that preacher's trash was still trash and had to be carried via elevator to the basement for hauling away.

Now the elevator would've won first prize at an antique show. It was more like a topless cage with all the pulleys and cables in full view. It was spooky looking and had a bad case of the shudders. Even with the Lord and my trash, I felt insecure. Those rides were as enjoyable as exploring a haunted house.

Renowned author-professor Wayne Oates convinced me that there's a difference between real and imaginary fear. Both have to be faced. I nerved up to facing the monster that lurked between the basement and the top floor. I punched him in the buttons and made him take me up and down, up and down. I even looked straight overhead and watched those pulleys let out cables like giant spiders spinning their threads. Gradually, fear gave way to a measure of enjoyment. Only a measure, mind you. I found out the thing was friendly and had no intention of ending the budding career of a young preacher.

We got along famously the rest of the year. I'd ride anytime—during daylight. It seemed to take on a different personality at night. I decided I could get all the riding I needed when my faith didn't have to be pushed to the limit. Anyway, I figured a victory was won.

There's an elevating truth riding here. Fear is real. David said, "What time I am afraid, I will trust in thee" (Ps. 56:3). He didn't say we wouldn't ever be afraid. He said we can face our fears and trust in God to do something about them.

Even our fears can lift us nearer to God. Riding up with Him is great joy. He'll never let us down.

Helpers for Heavy Loads

The old mud-encrusted dump truck was laboring up the grade. Its heavy dirt load cut its speed to well below the limit. Following behind, I wanted to pass. The curves and double yellow lines said, "If you've got any sense, you won't." Valuing the gift of life, I didn't. But that didn't keep ol' impatience from stirring up my insides. Finally, the hinderance to my progress turned down another street, and I went on my way.

Upon reflection, a few thoughts got dumped in my mind that helped me truck down a different avenue.

First, a lot of folks are like that truck. They've been through the mud and are carrying heavier loads than anyone might know about. They're doing the best they can with what power they have to pull the hills. They may unintentionally get in someone's way, but they can't help it and will move out of the way the first chance they get. They would welcome a bit of help if they could get it.

Second, fellow travelers need to put themselves in the cab of the other fellow's truck. Cuts down on impatience's exhaust fumes. The desire to "pass by on the other side" gives way to a willingness to slow down, stay close, and help if you can.

Memories of some personal hill climbing will make one more tolerant of the struggling hill climber up ahead; might even bring to mind the face of someone whose eyes said, "I understand."

Like roads, life has grades from slight to steep, with curves in between. Nobody walks on the level and straight always. So it pays to be kind to the hurting, for our hurts are a'comin'—mental, spiritual, or physical. Sometimes in truck loads.

Being overloaded is tough cargo to haul. But the kindness we've shown to others will come back in our hill-pulling times.

Third, there's the invitation and promise given by Jesus. "Come unto me, all ye that labour and are heavy laden, and I will give you rest" (Matt. 11:28).

Folks can help one another, but there are times when we need something more. Jesus is that "Something More." He neither tailgates behind us, floorboards it around us, nor gets impatient toward us; He graciously rides with us.

By His power, "Every valley shall be exalted, and every mountain and hill shall be made low: and the crooked shall be made straight, and the rough places plain: And the glory of the Lord shall be revealed" (Isa. 40:4-5).

Jesus and tenderhearted helpers make heartbreak hill less severe for all.

6

Tall Truths from . . .
The Evidence
of the Grace of God

Punishment and Forgiveness

An elderly man had two perfectly smooth silver discs that he always carried in his pocket. A friend asked what they were. It turned out that they were silver dollars.

An unusual story was related.

When the man was a boy, his mother caught him taking two silver dollars out of her pocketbook. His punishment was to carry those dollars in his pocket as long as *she* lived. He'd carried them so long all of the inscriptions had worn off. He couldn't count the pockets he'd worn out, and he said he thought his mother would never die. She finally did at the age of 103.

Nearly all of his life he had carried those reminders of what he had done. He said, "Every time I look at them I know I'm not supposed to steal." He turned out to be a fine, upstanding citizen.

Now as effective as this punishment proved to be in one case, God has provided a way that reaches out to all. It's the costliest plan ever devised, and it works. Everybody is "caught" in sin whether or not one admits it. Admitting it can lead to repentance, and repentance sets God's plan in action.

At the heart of God's way of dealing with sin and the

sinner is the cross. The center cross on Mount Calvary's brow, the shadow of which covers all generations, is God's plan. It's the cross on which Jesus died. The Bible declares, "For he hath made him [Jesus] to be sin for us, who knew no sin; that we might be made the righteousness of God in him" (2 Cor. 5:21). "So Christ was once offered to bear the sins of many" (Heb. 9:28).

The Holy Spirit mercifully "discovers" our sins and lets us know we didn't get away with them. Being discovered, punishment is required. He points us to Jesus and the cross. The words "in whom we have redemption through his blood, the forgiveness of sins, according to the riches of his grace" (Eph. 1:7) strike home. Repenting, we find that our punishment was taken by Him. "Godly sorrow worketh repentance" (2 Cor. 7:10), and the Lord is gracious to the repentant. He doesn't require us to carry the sin with us or the guilt or anything to remind us of our wrong. Restitution is mandatory when possible, but the guilt is taken away.

To the forgiven, the thought of the cross is a constant reminder of God's love and His way of handling our sins. Then we can say, "Every time I look at the cross I know I'm not supposed to sin."

Since Jesus took our punishment, His forgiveness toward us is available. No need for us to carry even two dollars worth of punishment when He says, "Be of good cheer; thy sins be forgiven thee" (Matt. 9:2).

Amen.

A Dogged Bit of Truth

It was a strange sight at the receptionist's desk. On my way out of McPherson Hospital, a quick glance in that direction didn't fully register until I got outside. I decided to do a double take to see if what I thought I saw was what I had seen.

Sure enough, a rather unusual looking receptionist was looking back at me. The face was attractive, surrounded by long, wavy hair. The nose was long and pointed, but seemed just right for the face. The ears were quite large, capable of listening to all sorts of complaints. The eyes were soft brown, with a soulful expression.

Now what it was, was a dog. Yes, sir, there he stood, erect, with his paws on the desk and looking out through the window like he worked there. Was I relieved when the nice lady on duty explained that he belonged to one of the doctors! I thought for a minute my glasses needed changing.

If I had inquired of the "new employee" about a patient's condition, he probably would've said, "Ruff!" I was thinking, *What in the world are you doing here?* And the look on his face seemed to say, "Dogged if I know."

It's good that things are not always what they appear to be. In spite of misleading evidence, McPherson's had not gone to the dogs.

Many a person has "gone to the dogs" before God finds him and makes him the recipient of His love and grace. Jesus was all the time looking for such prospects.

Mary Magdalene was devil-infested. The record said she had seven evil spirits in her. That's a whole passel of the varmints. Jesus saw what she really was—a potential child of God. He exterminated the devils and caused her to be "a crown of glory in the hand of the Lord" (Isa. 62:3). She got to see Jesus first on His resurrection day (Mark 16:9). Without fear of contradiction, the "new" Mary must've been glad that Jesus had not written her off as "no good" when he first saw her. He never does.

No power on earth can turn a dog into a receptionist. But God can take the most unlikely of us and make us into something like Jesus. And that's an even greater miracle.

Chase that truth around awhile. You won't be barking up the wrong tree.

Faith, Love, and Faithfulness

What a memorable picture of devotion to the Lord and His church!

Lonnie Stone was ninety years old. Due to illness, his church attendance had been below his usual par. The desire was as strong as ever, but his legs weren't.

One Sunday morning the angels must've rejoiced and the Lord, no doubt, smiled. Maybe Lonnie's promised crown of righteousness took on added luster that day (see 2 Tim. 4:8).

Surrounded by family helpers, the aged Stone was coming to church. Daughter Elizabeth led the way, carrying his walker. Son-in-law Vance and nephew W. T. gave him support under each arm, measuring their steps according to his. Slowly they made their way to his beloved Sunday School class. Later he was helped to the auditorium. There he joined in the service, singing lustily as had been his custom for years.

Mr. Stone's hearing was less than sharp, limiting his

sermon intake. But his presence declared whose side he was on. By overcoming all obstacles, he was saying, "My heart is here and so am I." He made an indelible mark on our hearts that day. Beautiful!

The Bible says, "Be thou faithful unto death, and I will give thee a crown of life" (Rev. 2:10). I have a notion that that crown will be mighty becoming to that hoary head. The Lord puts a premium on faithfulness. If He required measurable success, some of us would come out on the short end of the stick. According to man's judging, our accomplishments may be about as visible as electricity. But who can tell what God is doing through His quiet, faithful servants?

The business world says success is being at the right place at the right time. How much more true this is when applied to God's work. Success, in His dictionary, is spelled *faithfulness.*

I've known people who would probably forget their own names if called on to pray aloud. Some would as soon jump off of the church steeple as speak up in business meeting. But many of these same folks are as faithful to the church as the rising of the sun. Their love for the Lord is as deep as the sea. Without them the church would have about as much strength as an army without soldiers.

Jesus changed Simon's name to Peter—meaning stone or rock. He said He would build His church upon the rock of Peter's confession of faith (Matt. 16:18). Hard rock Simon Peter became a cornerstone of the church.

Lonnie Stone's determined faith was a chip off the old rock. And the Lord has need for a rock pile.

Mom's Contagious Faith

A mother is one of God's finest ideas. I don't know how we'd get here without one. She has the awesome task of heading her offspring in the right direction. Of course, she should have some help from her mate, but her role is special.

In heaven's providence, I was blessed to be given to a good mom. As far back as memory serves, her faith has been as deep as a well. Reaches all the way down to the source of life—God. She instilled in her children a knowledge and love for Jesus and the things He loves.

My enduring love for the church was transmitted by her. She took us to church and Jesus finally took hold in our hearts. Young folks sat near the back of the auditorium, adults farther down. Sometimes we'd misbehave and Mom would look around. All she had to do was clear her throat. I knew that sound very well. It was time to settle down. She was saying, "The Lord is in his holy temple" (Hab. 2:20), and there's a time to be silent before Him. Reverence for Jesus was what she wanted me to learn.

She combines common sense with faith. More locks are on the doors than Houdini could pick, plus a cactus plant under a window to let a would-be intruder get the point. Living alone, after Dad died, her confidence in God's protective care was demonstrated. One night she was awakened by a noise and could not go back to sleep. As she lay in bed, a Scripture filled her mind: "Behold, he that keepeth Israel shall neither slumber nor sleep" (Ps. 121:4). She knew that means that God watches over His own. She said, "I didn't see any reason for both of us to stay awake, so I decided to go to sleep and let God do the watching."

She trusts God to care for her in the daytime as well. Even in her eighties she is an active cosmetics saleslady. Several years ago she had been walking the hot streets of Louisville, delivering orders. Being home on vacation, I expressed concern about her working during the long, hot summertime. With a sense of humor which has served her well, she said: "You'd be surprised at what a breeze you can stir up if you walk fast."

Active faith is more caught than taught. Mothers, with a good case of contagious Christianity, can be the cause of their children coming up with it. Who knows; it could even turn into an epidemic.

Postscript

Mom's faith was the never-failing kind—the kind that God honors. She prayed to be spared from suffering and helplessness when departing time drew near. She also prayed that she would never have to move out of her beloved little home of fifty years.

She experienced no pain at all, but because of a general weakness in her body, she entered the hospital on Tuesday, March 30. Saturday, April 3, 1982 became her coronation day. She loved good fun and joked with the nurses. She loved good food and enjoyed some ice cream. She loved pretty flowers and named each flower in the bouquet brought by her grandson, Larry Dale, who was born on her birthday. She loved him dearly and told him how glad she was that he came to see her. She loved the Lord supremely, who was at hand calling her. And she put her head on her pillow and died. Beautiful.

She ran with patience the race that was set before her, "Looking unto Jesus, the author and finisher of our [her] faith" (Heb. 12:2).

A Strange Counter Encounter

A chance meeting with a total stranger can sometimes take an unexpected turn. It makes you wonder how chancy it really was.

I met a young man at the counter of Stamey's Barbecue in Greensboro, North Carolina. Our small talk grew in dimensional meaning when we learned we both were Baptist Christians. We were spiritual kinfolks.

Mentioning that his company had sent him to Kentucky, my ears perked up. I said, "I'm from Kentucky. Where did you work?" "Around Middlesboro, Harlan, Corbin, and London," he answered. I told him my daddy came from that area, and I use to go there as a boy.

The conversation could've stopped there, but the best was yet to come.

He said, "I lived in a little place called Lily. It's between London and Corbin." Well, Sir, you could've knocked me off the stool with a hush puppy. Do I know where Lily is? You're mighty right I do. It figures in my being in the world.

I revealed some ancient history to my new counter friend. Growing up in the Kentucky mountains, my dad was known to tote a gun and have a rowdy spell at times. Lily had the dubious honor of his company one night about seventy years ago. What the provocation was, I don't know; but he shot up the place. Got himself run out of town and headed for Louisville. Having no desire to eyeball the sheriff, years passed before he returned. The charges had been dropped.

How strange that of all the people in North Carolina a person with connections in Lily, Kentucky, should sit next to me. A chain of thoughts linked up in my mind.

Had Dad not shot up Lily, he wouldn't have fled to Louisville. Had he not gone to Louisville, he wouldn't have met Ina Crenshaw. Had they not met, I would never have been born. Makes me plumb glad that Dad had encouragement to hightail it out of the mountains and head for the city.

There's one more "had not." Had Dad not made peace with God through Jesus Christ, his body wouldn't be resting in peace in a Laurel County mountain cemetery awaiting the resurrection of the saved. But he had, long ago.

Treasured letters from him assure me that Jesus lived in his heart. He said, "I know if anything happens to me, God will take care of me. I put that matter in His hands a long time ago, and I want you all to know that no day passes that I don't ask Him to be with me, and I know He is."

From shooting up a town called Lily to knowing Jesus, the Lily of the Valley. What a journey!

Ode to "Miss Teeny"

My sweet mother-in-law, Teeny Congleton, is a happy resident of the Baptist Home in Hamilton, North Carolina. Physically she does pretty well, but Alzheimer's debilitating effect keeps exacting its toll. Her loving spirit is alive and well, her faith in the Heavenly Father is beautifully intact, and her reverence for the Bible and prayer will bless the visitor's heart.

Recently, two daughters and husbands went to see "Miss Teeny." Before leaving, Scripture was read and prayer was offered. Her attempted commentary on the Scripture was not as clear as the desire to comment; but God understood. At the prayer's conclusion, she said, "That was a good prayer. Bless your heart." And four hearts got blessed.

On the wall there hangs a beautiful portrait of her in her twenties. Dressed in the style of that day, and a hairdo in keeping with the times, one could well understand why "Pa" chose and married such a belle.

Seated in her easy chair, beneath the picture reminiscent of a bygone era, a blending of years unfolded—beautiful blending.

I looked first at the likeness of a pretty, smiling, vivacious, clear-eyed, dark-haired girl with a rose petal complexion. Then I looked at the still pretty, still smiling, eighty-year-old great grandmother.

Now she is able to walk only a few steps at a time, her eyes are clouded with loss of memory, her hair is white and no longer abundant, and the rose petal complexion is gently faded and lined with age. And as I looked at her sitting there, I remembered something.

I remembered a lovely statement by the late Vance Havner, veteran prophet of God. He told of his thoughts when he sat by the bedside of his disease-wracked wife of many years. "I remembered how she used to look. I saw how she looked now. And I thought of how she is going to look someday." What an expression of the Christian faith! Unbeatable.

And that Bible-inspired view of life paraded through my mind like a sunbeam breaking through a misty cloud.

There were the two Teenys—past and present. But a span of time intermingled with Jesus' gift to her of eternal life. Exquisite beauty, flawless beauty await her. At the sound of His gentle beckoning call, whenever, she will ascend to her full becoming.

A beam of light from God's lighthouse says, "Beloved, now are we the sons [children] of God, and it doth not yet appear what we shall be: but we know that, when he [Jesus] shall appear, we shall be like him; for we shall see him as he is" (1 John 3:2).

I remembered, I saw, I thought. And that day heaven and earth kissed each other.

Glory be!

Permanent Metamorphosis

"For the Lord taketh pleasure in his people: he will beautify the meek with salvation" (Ps. 149:4). That must mean a saved person changes from ugly to pretty. A spiritual metamorphosis takes place. The word means "any complete change in appearance, character, or circumstances." And when it happens inside, it's as apt to show outwardly as when a caterpillar dresses up in butterfly garb.

Uncle Lester was a Kentucky mountain man. He was big, tough as jerky, a road builder, a man's man. Like E. F. Hutton, when he talked you listened. He had cold, steely blue eyes that could drill through you like an auger. His countenance was stern like the mountain winters.

As a boy, I would visit in Uncle Lester's home in summertime. He bedded and boarded me, providing some happy childhood memories in his beloved Kentucky mountains. I learned to love the mountains, but I had an awesome respect for him.

Years passed. As a man I saw him again. Bless my soul, he had gotten himself metamorphosed! I had never seen such a change. He was about as much like his old self as Paul was like Saul before the light hit him on the Damascus road (Acts 9:1-16).

There was a gentleness about him, a softened expression, eyes without fierceness, in his tongue was the law of kindness and a lovableness that put you at ease. What in the world had happened? Actually, it was something from out of this world. He told his story.

The church was having a revival. He said, "A couple of Methodist preachers came to see me and led me to the Lord. I accepted Christ and joined the church." It's like the verse that says, "Thou hast made known to me the ways of life; thou shalt make me full of joy with thy countenance" (Acts 2:28). He didn't know that Scripture, but that's what happened to him.

Then he added something that still echoes in my heart: "I'll never know why I served the devil all of those years." Of course, he didn't. Nobody who does can ever explain why. It sounded for the world like he'd found himself a new Master to serve. He had, and gave evidence of it thereafter. Talking about the Lord came easy and natural like it should for those who "have passed from death unto life" (1 John 3:14). The devil had about as much hold on him after Jesus took over as a man has on a greased pig.

Metamorphosis of the heart always shows on the face. The Bible says of the time some folks looked at Stephen, "Looking steadfastly on him, [they] saw his face as it had been the face of an angel" (Acts 6:15).

Uncle Lester and Stephen became brothers. And there's room in God's family for more.

Down, But Not Out

I stood by the bedside of a real man. Over forty years ago he was a paratrooper in the European war theater. Having survived in the battle for our freedom, he became a craftsman of fine furniture at Y and J Furniture Company. Several years ago he was felled by a stroke.

A man's relationship with God is of paramount importance. During the early years of confinement, his quest for the assurance of salvation led to the high plateau of peace through the Lord Jesus Christ. He and the Lord became intimate friends.

Another stroke robbed him of the use of the left side of his body; a nursing home became his home. Acceptance of his unsought condition and his cheerful spirit wreathed in smiles and laughter brightened the lives of attendants and visitors.

Recently, came stroke number three. But, unlike strike number three, he is down, but not out. He is completely helpless from shoulders to toes. Movement of head, clarity of speech, and mind remain—and a wholeness of spirit coupled with an unshakable faith in God. Having passed through a limited valley of depression, the old sparkle has returned. His physical world has been reduced to a corner of a room, but there's a light in that corner.

When a man has faith, he doesn't live "under the circumstances" but on top of them. There's no bitterness in this guy's heart and no resentment against God. He doesn't understand the why of it all, but he has long since heard God whisper to his heart, "My grace is sufficient for thee: for my strength is made perfect in weakness" (2 Cor. 12:9).

Dependence on God's Word is the mark of a reverent

and trusting heart. He has asked his daughter to inscribe the twenty-third Psalm in large calligraphic letters. Among his pictures and plaques, this will hang at the foot of his bed. Always available to his eyes and heart will be, among others, the words of the psalmist: "The Lord is my shepherd. . . . Yea, though I walk through the valley of the shadow of death, I will fear no evil: for thou art with me. . . . Surely goodness and mercy shall follow me all the days of my life: and I will dwell in the house of the Lord for ever."

Concerning the future life, there awaits this godly man the resurrection's promise: the body "is sown in weakness; it is raised in power" (1 Cor. 15:43). He looks up, out, and beyond.

Thurman George, I salute you with all the gratitude, admiration, and respect that salute includes. You are a real man, a man in Christ.

7

Tall Truths from . . .
Being Aware of Who We Are

Footprints

Whenever you feel high and mighty, take a walk on the beach. Splash along where the spent waves take a swipe at the land. Make some footprints and watch what happens. It'll deflate your ego like a rubber raft attacked by a swordfish.

As I perambulated along the beach I watched the water lick my feet, then turn and run seaward. (May be why it turned and ran.) Between waves, my footprints were visible. After another wave would roll in and retreat, I'd wonder how I got where I was. No more footprints in sight than a ghost would've left. I had made about as lasting an imprint on the soggy sand as one of those skinny-legged beach birds does.

Perhaps prominent people promenaded by. Not knowing their accomplishments, I was unimpressed with their tootsie tracks. So was the ocean.

Maybe a few peacock-proud folks strutted along, leaving little more than turkey tracks behind. These, too, were all washed away.

Parabolically the ocean was saying, "Man's earthly life is about as permanent as the white caps on my waves."

There's one exception to all of this. Jesus! He made

footprints so deep in the earth they will last forever. Wherever He walked, people knew He had been there. He walked with even steps, uprightly, always going about doing good. He walked right into the hearts of those who loved Him and believed Him. He still does.

His most famous, terrible, and terribly necessary footprints were made between a crooked court and a cruel cross. They became indelible in history and eternity. But His prints cannot be seen around the foot of the cross. He was up on it. There He fulfilled His promise, "And I, if I be lifted up from the earth, will draw all men unto me" (John 12:32). Our salvation was complete.

He had also said, "He that followeth me shall not walk in darkness, but shall have the light of life" (John 8:12). By following Jesus, mortal tracks become immortal. Saints alive!

Oblivion may be the destiny of our footprints in man's mind. Not so with God, if we have walked to the foot of the cross, and knelt. For "He withdraweth not his eyes from the righteous" (Job 36:7), and "The steps of a good man are ordered by the Lord" (Ps. 37:23). God takes notice of how, when, and where we walk, and remembers.

If we walk with Jesus on earth, it may be said of us as it was of Enoch, "Enoch walked with God: and he was not; for God took him" (Gen. 5:24).

Cast a meditative hook in this ocean of truth. You'll get more than a nibble.

Pins for Pride's Balloons

Pride makes a man forget who he really is. It can sneak up on you like a "cat burglar" and grab you before you know it. Being stuck on yourself puts a good deal of distance between you and God. The Bible says, "The proud he knoweth afar off" (Ps. 138:6). Makes talking with the Lord a long-distance call.

Getting puffed up with self-importance may take awhile; deflation is like popping a balloon with a pin. God uses a variety of pins.

I had taken a copy of my book *Out of the Crate* into a nursing home for a possible sale. I was sure those elderly folks would appreciate all of that humor. Sure enough, the director thought it a worthwhile library addition.

Coming in from the bright sunlight, I had not removed my dark sun shades. There I stood, with that mysterious "Who is he?" "What's he done?" look. Haughtiness was about to swell me up. I forgot the warning, "Pride goeth before destruction, and an haughty spirit before a fall" (Prov. 16:18). It was on the brink of happening.

The unfamous author was leaning importantly against the door facing. An unimpressed resident noticed only one thing—the dark glasses. With apparent concern she said, "You blind?" It's amazing how fast you can reenter the real world. Here was a person with more pity than admiration. I neither needed the one nor deserved the other. I fell as flat as a hoarse soloist trying to reach high C.

Was I blind? You bet. Pride is like a blindfold that shuts out reality. The Bible says, "If a man think himself to be something, when he is nothing, he deceiveth himself"

(Gal. 6:3). It's as easy to be deceived as it is to fall into a hole on a moonless night. And pride is a hole.

Ol' King Nebuchadnezzar got a bad case of "I" trouble. Thought he'd done some real great things by his own power for his own majesty. God made him eat grass like an ox, and his hair grew until it looked like eagles' feathers, and his nails like birds' claws. A right sad comedown for a king. When he learned his lesson, his senses and his kingdom were returned to him. Then he praised the King of heaven and said, "Those that walk in pride he is able to abase" (Dan. 4:37). Verily, He does.

One long, contemplative look at the cross of Jesus shrivels pride. And "The Lord hath respect unto the lowly" (Ps. 138:6).

Eating a good dish of crow is good for the soul.

Profitable Rebuking

"Rebuke a wise man, and he will love thee" (Prov. 9:8). At least one time in my life I qualified as wise. My wife rebuked me when I needed it, and later, I loved her for it. Being rebuked is about as pleasant to the rebukee as a spur is to a horse; but when rightly applied, it produces results.

I had a soul sickness. The kind that eats you up on the inside. Failing to admit it or label it made it grow like putting Vigaro on a plant. My words, unbeknownst to me, enabled "Dr." Harriett to diagnose my case. It was called S.O.J. Real serious, with deadly effects.

Now the cause of this malady was the attitude I had toward a fellow preacher. Our friendship went back to college and seminary days, but he had outdistanced me. His mind was tack sharp, he graduated with honors and had the audacity to wear his Phi Beta Kappa key. Not only that, he had a bigger church than my two half-time ones put together and was moving along right conspiciously. What was a fellow whose self-esteem was about as high as a kite on the ground to do? Why, tear him apart, naturally. Behind his back, of course. My wife was the sounding board for the keen observations I made of this accomplished brother's faults. I skinned and dissected him like a toad frog in a zoology lab. Didn't have sense enough to know I was skinning myself, and he was unscathed. Fact is, he was about as conscious of my feelings as a preacher is of some people's real intentions who join the church.

I reckon the Lord and Harriett finally had enough of the picayunish prattling, so they spoke. I heard both voices even though He used my wife's soft-speaking, uncondemning voice. As I unloaded a fresh barrage, she said, "I think you are suffering from the sin of jealousy." S.O.J. Now why did she have to say that! And that's all she said as she turned and walked away. There I stood with the inside of my heart as exposed as a thief in the light of a lawman's five-cell flashlight.

The gracious Lord didn't take me to the woodshed but to the closet. There we had a talk. We agreed that the garbage of jealousy needed shoveling out of my heart. When I called it by the right name, the Lord knew what to do with it. It was part of the "all sin" that "the blood of Jesus cleanseth us from" (1 John 1:7). As the sin disappeared, the suffering ceased. I was healed.

Later I talked with my "brother" about it and told him what the Lord had done. Our friendship deepened, and I discovered what God does with another servant is just plain none of my business.

The "Green-Eyed-Monster" is just that—a monster. Beware lest he take a ride on your back.

Confidence and Preservation

A proper evaluation of self is proper. The Bible says one is "not to think of himself more highly than he ought to think" (Rom. 12:3). I reckon the flip side of that would be not to think more lowly, either.

Two happenings in seven-year-old Valerie Albright's school days illustrate the principle.

A little girl in her class was given more math homework than she. Her mother asked, "Valerie, is it because she is better in math than you are?" She answered, "Yes, but I can do some things better than she can." Score one for self-confidence.

The other event had to do with report card time. Bringing home her first "C" ever, her mother was a mite upset. "Valerie, what is the meaning of this 'C' "? Uh-oh! A real touchy situation. Quick wittedly she said, "I think it means *congratulations!*" Score one for self-preservation.

The good Lord doesn't want us to think of ourselves as nobodies or too much somebodies. But true self-confidence comes when our confidence is in Him. "For the Lord shall be thy confidence" (Prov. 3:26). And true preservation comes by being "preserved in Jesus Christ" (Jude 1).

The Lord told Moses to get himself down to Egypt and tell ol' Pharaoh that his Israelite slaves were to hie themselves to Canaan land. Kinda startled him. His self-confidence was about mole-hill high. He protested, "Who am

I that I should go unto Pharaoh?" God said, "Certainly I will be with thee." Moses: "I am slow of speech, and of a slow tongue." God: "I will be with thy mouth, and teach thee what thou shalt say" (Ex. 3:11-12; 4:10,12). Now brother Aaron could do some things better than Moses; but what God wanted done, only Moses could do.

Well, Sir, the future lawgiver got himself some confidence, went, eyeballed Egypt's lord and told him what the real Lord wanted done. Led a crowd bigger than a politician could count from slavery to freedom. He learned to think of himself as his enabling God thought of him.

Self-preservation begins when a person realizes old self will self destruct but a new self is indestructable. And the New Self Giver says to the seeking soul, "What is the meaning of that 'F' in your life?" Comes the honest answer, "It really means 'Failure,' but I want it to mean 'Faith.'" In comes Jesus, with grace, and makes it so (Eph. 2:8). "Congratulations!" shout the angels.

The Bible says, "The Lord preserveth all them that love him" (Ps. 145:20).

From self-confidence to confidence in God; from self-preservation to preservation in God!

Think highly of that.

Be Who You Are

Knowing and admitting who we are makes it easier to live with ourselves. Trying to be something we're not makes a person strain under a heavy load. It's like a Mack truck with a Honda engine, going uphill. To find out who lives inside this skin of ours and work with him is more sensible. The discovery may humble us and prod us toward our true destinies.

Jesus said we have to become as little children to enter the kingdom (Matt. 18:3). That's not regressing but progressing. A little child can put us deluded older folks to shame with his honesty. Daniel Hopkins, when three, is a case in point.

Dressed up in his softball uniform, he attended a game. Afterwards, he found the field a good place to play. Someone asked him, "Whose team are you on?" (Sounds like something a grown-up would say.) Having no delusions of grandeur, his reply was as solid as a home run. His slight lisp came through when he said, "I'm juth a little kid." Made it sound like anybody with common sense should have known that.

The Bible says a person is "not to think of himself more highly than he ought to think" (Rom. 12:3). This was written by Paul, a man who was as proud as a strutting rooster before he met Jesus. The vision he had of the Lord cleared his vision of himself. Later he admitted "I am chief sinner" (see 1 Tim. 1:15). Knowing that he was a plain old sinner, saved by grace, made him as usable as a light'ard knot for kindling a fire. He'd climbed down off his high horse.

David, as a boy, was to fight braggart Goliath, who was a shade over nine feet tall. Dressed in King Saul's armor, David must've felt about as right as a hobo in a tuxedo. He said, "I cannot go with these; for I have not proved them" (1 Sam. 17:39). And he took the stuff off. In the vernacular, he was saying, "I'm juth a little kid." Then David, as David, and not a miniature Saul, popped Goliath in the forehead with a rock that made the not-so-genial-giant fall on his face with an earth-shaking thud. David had told him,

"I come to thee in the name of the Lord" (v. 45). Didn't make much impression on him, but the "slang" stone did. David was his own self, a "stripling" (v. 56); but he stripped Goliath of his head.

The Bible warns, "If a man thinketh himself to be something, when he is nothing, he deceiveth himself" (Gal. 6:3). But there's always a place of service for those whose spirit is that of "juth a little kid."

Bird Talk

It still rings in my memory: "A little bird told me." I hated that sound and wished many times I could have set a snare for that tattletale. It would've been pure pleasure to wring his neck.

Years passed before I learned that that evasive answer mothers use on their sneaky younguns is biblical. Yes Sir, ol' King Solomon penned it: "Curse not the king, no not in thy thought; and curse not the rich in thy bedchamber: for a bird of the air shall carry the voice, and that which hath wings shall tell the matter" (Eccl. 10:20).

I remember a day in grammar school. I think it was the time the teacher made me stand out in the hall for some infraction of the rules. (That's when they had rules you could infract.) I had as much intention of telling my mother about it as a moonshiner has of locating his still for revenuers.

Mom met me at school that day. I came out of the classroom, looking as pleasant as a kid with a deep dark secret locked up inside could. Her greeting made my feathers fall: "What happened to you today?" After confessing, I asked her how she knew. "A little bird told me," she said. Drat that bird! Either he got around a lot or he was one of a covey of the blabber beaks. A foul break.

Sometimes a human voice is used. In this case the big-mouth bird's name was Joe. He flew out of the room and perched by my mother before I got to her, then flew away. I thought he was my buddy; but to me, he was kin to Benedict Arnold.

Didn't seem fair that my well-being was in double jeopardy—by my teacher and my mother.

That wasn't the last time a "bird of gossip" chirped on someone. Why the whole world must be bugged with such birds. You do something wrong, and before you can say, "I didn't do it," somebody knows that you did.

Gradually, I learned you can't do wrong and get by. This goes back to another infallible truth: "Be sure your sin will find you out" (Num. 32:23). The thing will hunt us down like Sherlock Holmes. Relentlessly it stalks us and finally says, "This is your sin!" Fits like a tailor-made suit.

Sin finds us out in what it does to us personally—harming us in body, soul, and spirit. It screams in our conscience like a banshee. It disgraces us in the eyes of friends. It judges us guilty in the sight of God.

But that "little bird" turns out to be a friend. He helps us to know the truth about ourselves. "For nothing is secret, that shall not be made manifest; neither any thing hid, that shall not be known and come abroad" (Luke 8:17). If our sins are uncovered in time, Jesus, who took them upon Himself (1 Pet. 2:24), will cover them for us for eternity.

If we're smart enough to listen to the truth, we won't sound like a cuckoo on judgment day.

A Hairy Story

There are times when a pair of eyes in the back of our heads would be helpful. Not only could we see where we've been, but a rear view might help us in self-improvement. Could cut down on some giggling behind our backs by others, too.

Bill Goss is a tall, fine-looking man with white, wavy hair. He keeps it well groomed and is the kind of man who stands out in a crowd. One day he stood out more than he realized and later wished he'd stayed at home.

He was all dressed up to attend a funeral. His freshly laundered hair was a bit unruly in the back and needed pasting down. Irene, his obliging wife, sat him down on a stool and shot a little hair spray on the waving waves. Thinking himself presentable, he sashayed off to join the solemn company of mourners and pay his respects to the deceased.

Now funerals are by nature not very smiley occasions. The urge to laugh has to be squelched if something tips over your guffaw box. Doubtless, Bill must've had the attention of the folks on the pews behind him. They were hard pressed to keep their pursed lips pursed.

Finally, a young girl asked a question that would shake any red-blooded man down to his toes. She said, "Do you know you have some hair clips on the back of your head?" Yes, Sir, unbeknown to Bill, Irene had put in a couple of big, long aluminum clips to hold his hair in place until the spray dried. Only trouble though, she forgot about them and Bill never knew about them until the awful moment of truth.

The funeral service continued, with the preacher having no way of knowing what a hairy situation had arisen. Bill sat there, perhaps saying with the psalmist, "Innumerable evils have compassed me about. . . . I am not able to look up; they are more than the hairs of mine head: therefore my heart faileth me. Be pleased, O Lord, to deliver me: O Lord, make haste to help me" (Ps. 40:12-13).

Back home, it was meet that the perpetrator of this embarrassment be faced. "Irene, do you know what you did to me?" Honestly and innocently she didn't. When informed, she said "I'm sorry." But then the impact of the whole scene hit her. Her apology was followed with a couple of giggles. After that she could no more keep from almost laughing her head off than a laughing-gassed dental patient could keep a long face.

They are still husband and wife, but I'll wager she'll never get within forty feet of him again with a spray can. Most likely, for precaution's sake, he rubs the back of his head before appearing in public and may even use a couple of mirrors to be sure.

At times we Christians have some mighty strange looking non-Christian practices clipped onto our lives. They make others gawk at us and laugh rather than gaze at the Savior in us and laud Him.

The Bible says, "Let a man examine himself" (1 Cor. 11:28). Self-examination can be real revealing, leading to correction. It cuts down on embarrassment to ourselves and to our Lord.

8

Tall Truths from . . .
Laughing with God

Man Forgets; God Does, Too

Memory is the power to reproduce what has been learned or experienced. At times we forget what we are trying to remember. Then we're left holding a stem of a thought without so much as a bud of truth to show. Can be sort of a thorny situation.

Dr. Allen Easley blocked a near untimely exit from Wake Forest College for me with this jim-dandy piece of wisdom: "Sometimes it's better to stay and master a situation than to let the situation master you." That took root in my mind and has been shared times aplenty.

Now a sermon I was preaching had just the right spot for emphasizing perseverance and overcoming. Aiming to quote my friend who helped salvage my college career, I confidently began, "I'll never forget something Dr. Easley said." Then the thing got as tangled in my mind as hair that hadn't been combed in a month. I gave it a try or two and messed it up real good. I don't even remember what I finally said, but it made as much sense as reciting poetry backwards.

Then there was the time I was preaching on "light." All kinds of truth were shining through. Several bright points had illuminated the minds of those eager listeners, but I had one more shaft to beam on them. So I said, "And another thing light will do _____" There I stood, mouth open and ready, in utter darkness. My mind was as full of light as Mammoth Cave before it was discovered. A blank memory matched the look on my face. The sermon outline was snickering in my coat pocket, so I shot from the hip. It was the most profound ray of all: "Light will do a lot of things." And I proceeded to other startling utterances.

Forgetfulness may embarrass us, but the Bible reveals God's merciful capacity to forget. To those who abide safely in Christ, He makes this heart-gladdening promise: "Their sins and their iniquities will I remember no more" (Heb. 8:12).

Like one devout brother prayed, "O Lord, separate our sins from us as far as the east is from the west, and throw 'em in the sea of forgetness!" (see Ps. 103:12; Mic. 7:19). And He does.

Don't forget to remember God!

Miracle Pill

Hearing only a part of a statement can conjure up some right strange thoughts. Professor Johnson, Southern Seminary's famous speech teacher, verified this with a story which sounded something like this.

A tardy worshiper entered the church vestibule at anthem-rendering time. It was a four-part bit of harmony. Each section would do its part separately and then put them together. The latecomer couldn't see the group but was a mite unnerved at what he heard. The sopranos screeched, "I want to take a pill." The supportive altos echoed, "I want to take a pill." The tenors agreed they wanted one, and the basses bellowed out they had to have one, too. Poor fellow must've thought they were sicker than they sounded. He was about to back out of the meeting house, sure that an epidemic was raging. Just then the singers got the whole thing lined up and joyfully made some sense out of it: "I want to take a pil-grim journey."

To the relieved brother's notion, that was a sight better than pill taking. It may have enticed him to go wherever the pil-grims were heading.

It pays to hear a person out. A seeker might miss going on the heavenly journey if he thinks he has to gulp a pill to get there.

'Course now, there is a pill that's a wonder-worker for sure. It's been on the market for centuries. All the cost of it was paid a long time ago, so it's free for the taking.

Put it inside a spiritually dead man, and he'll get up prancin' all over the place. Folks, with big, invisible loads strapped to their backs, take one and stand up straight like something just fell off. It does wonders for furrowed brows, and it'll mend hearts that got broken all to pieces.

Other benefits are noticeable. It will freshen a foul-word mouth like spray deodorizer freshens a foul-smelling room. One good dose, taken by a fellow with a disposition like a cobra, will gentle him like a lamb. And it has curative power for those diseases that eat us up on the inside—hate, envy, lust, plus a host of others.

Miracles appear when the whole family takes the prescription. Homes become outposts of heaven. Dads turn into dandy ones. Moms modify mightily for good. And children take on a cherubic character.

The name of this elixir is GOSPILL - pronounced gospel. It's taken, not by mouth, but by heart. A full dose makes a new person out of us on earth and fixes us so we live forever.

The gospel is Jesus. "And this is the record, that God hath given to us eternal life, and this life is in his Son" (1 John 5:11). "Jesus Christ maketh thee whole" (Acts 9:34).

He's the best medicine in the world!

Strange Refrain

Ordinarily, heavenly and earthly things are thought to be somewhat removed from each other. Sometimes they get mighty close together, and strange things result.

The morning worship service was on the verge of concluding. It was one of those times when the Lord made Himself real amongst us. Sniffles and tears mingled to confirm heaven's nearness. Most folks seemed glad they didn't miss that one. It was kinda like a good drenching rain on a parched parcel of land.

The preacher's heart got as tender as stall-fed beef. In the closing prayer, he was pleading with the Lord to move the moved to a deeper commitment of themselves to Him. The words were sorta aimed at the pews as well as to the ramparts of heaven—hoping for some ground to be gained for good.

Now the devil is as crouched and ready to spring as a peeved panther. Being on the alert, he must've been responsible for the local radio station's program coming through the church's sound system. There the preacher stood, beseeching as best he knew how, and found himself praying against the background of a lady country-western singer. Guitars and all. Not loud but loud enough to make you wonder what was going on.

That in itself might not sound too disconcerting, but the song wasn't what you'd call sacred, and would be hard to find in the hymnal. "I'm gonna stand by my man" wafted all around the auditorium. It has something to do with promising to stand together wherever and no matter what. The sentiment of the record has a poor track record in life. It's called breaking promises.

Pondering the matter, there's a striking resemblance to some of our commitments to the Lord. The altar call being issued, something moved us. May have been a "tearjerker," told with pathos by the preacher. Could've been a sentimental song that twanged the heartstrings. Whatever, we told the Lord we wanted to stand with Him. But when we found out where, it didn't especially suit us. That's when we too often reneged and left Him standing by Himself. I reckon He wasn't too surprised. Just disappointed.

The Bible says, "God is able to make him stand" (Rom. 14:4). That should keep us "Standing on the Promises" instead of vacating the premises.

If some stray music filters through again, I hope it will be, "Who is on the Lord's side? . . . . By Thy grace divine, We are on the Lord's side, Saviour, we are Thine." We might go out singing, "I'm gonna stand by my Lord!"

Double Vision

Hearing a statement and seeing an object can create an association in our minds. We are reminded of something —either good, bad, or, at times, surprising. It can be a mite unsettling if you happen to be the object of comparison in the unexpected association.

It happened in a revival. I laid a profoundly descriptive sentence on a certain kind of sinner: "He's as crooked as a dog's hind leg." That leaves little to the imagination and is designed to strike conviction in a less than honest heart. I said it and passed on to other profoundities.

The next night I learned that the reference to a canine's limb moved a thoughtful lady to action. It always gladdens a preacher's heart to know someone was listening.

She said, "Last night you said something about a person being as crooked as a dog's hind leg." "Yessum," said I, waiting with bated breath to hear the rest. "Well," she continued, "I never thought of a dog's leg being crooked, so I went home and looked at my dog's leg. Sure enough it is." That was straight truth about a crooked subject.

Doubtless what she learned was enlightening but nothing to howl about. I wish she had stopped there, but she wasn't finished. In all candor she added, "Everytime I look at that dog, I think of you." Wouldn't that bark your ego!

Now it's not uncommon to be told you remind someone of someone. But in this case I had that hangdog feeling. Didn't know whether to pity the dog or myself, for suddenly the preacher had gone to the dogs. I sure am glad she didn't reverse the associational order of things.

That bit of doggerel prose has a spiritual counterpart. Temporal things have a way of reminding us of things eternal. Look at a Bible and we think of God. A cross brings salvation to mind. A church spire lifts our thoughts toward heaven. And, amazingly, an unassuming Christian often reminds someone of the Lord Jesus Christ.

Peter and John spoke so well of Jesus the listeners saw more than a couple of men. The record says, "They took knowledge of them, that they had been with Jesus" (Acts 4:13). What a compliment!

Wonder what the world would be like if folks would listen to and look at all Christians and could say of each one, "That person makes me think of Jesus."

It was said of John the Baptist, "And the two disciples heard him speak, and they followed Jesus" (John 1:37). That's how it's meant to be.

Mulish Christians

A mule has the reputation of being stubborn, hardheaded, and a kicker. His strength as a load mover is often overshadowed by his more notorious traits. Thus, when a person is compared to a mule, a compliment is not the usual intention. Still, a mule has a place in the scheme of things that makes his being worthwhile.

A bit of autobiography reveals what thoughts may have been plodding around in the head of a certain "mule trainer."

Being diabetic, I explained to my wife that doctors tell me they get insulin from hogs and cows. (That in itself makes you wonder who your kin are.)

Now my "Lord, I'll help make him humble" helpmate has a penchant for occasional good-natured needling. Said

she, "I thought they got yours from a mule." Her impish
grin kept me from braying like one.

The Bible says, "Be ye not as the horse, or as the mule,
which have no understanding: whose mouth must be held
in with bit and bridle, lest they come near unto thee" (Ps.
32:9). Maybe my muleheadedness was more noticeable
than realized. Couldn't help but wonder if my observing
wife wasn't trying to tell me something.

Since I had become stablemate to a dumb beast, I felt
bound to twist this donkey tale into something paraboli-
cal. I decided some mulishness could be an asset. In at
least three ways.

First: Christians ought to have a stubbornness against
doing wrong. Like Joseph when he was bombarded by
Potiphar's roving-eyed wife to sin. "How then can I do
this great wickedness, and sin against God?" he asked his
temptress. He "fled, and got him out" (Gen. 39:9,12).
Godly stubbornness.

Second: A hardheaded biblical conviction of who Jesus
is is a commendable bit of mulishness. When it was revealed to Peter that Jesus is "the Christ, the Son of the
living God" (Matt. 16:16), nobody could "turn away his
ears from the truth" (2 Tim. 4:4). He was adamant about
the Lord through his dying day.

Third: Kicking is not always bad. Depends on what
you're kicking. Paul was notorious in kicking against Jesus
and the church until he met the Lord (Acts 9:1-9,20).
Probably he realized what a first-class, oversized donkey
he had been. Afterwards, with his head turned toward his
new Master, he spent the balance of his days kicking the
devil out of hearts and churches. From the record, he
could kick like a mule. And Satan has some bruises to show
for it.

Maybe some shots of refined mule insulin would do all of us some good.

Outards and Innards

"Man looketh on the outward appearance, but the Lord looketh on the heart" (1 Sam. 16:7). That's grounds for rejoicing, 'cause a fellow is not necessarily what we might judge him to be. His interior may be wrapped up in a misleading exterior. Not having x-ray vision, we snap judge by what we see first. We may not even come close to truth.

The Holy Land trip was over. Lots of huggin' and kissin' took place among the reunited at the airport. My unsuspecting wife was in for a shock. Looking at me, she squealed, "Crate, you didn't!" But, yes, I did. I hadn't shaved since departing two weeks earlier. I always had a hankering to grow a beard, but the accepted parson image hindered the doing. I jumped on the chance like a snappin' turtle after his prey. But my slow-growing whiskers didn't have that well-groomed, finished look and were dapple-gray, too.

Now my attempt to resemble Lincoln was met with several remarks. They put me in a class not fit for a respectable reverend. Harriett said, "You look dirty." Someone else chimed in, "You look like an old man." Another added 'em together: "You look like a dirty old man." They hurt my feelings something terrible. Here I was fresh from the Lord's land and judged like a rank sinner. Anyhow, my slightly stunned wife seemed to get a kick out of kissing "the dirty old man." I really hadn't changed at all. I just looked different.

Many a man is categorized, criticized, and ostracized because of bushy beards or lengthy locks. But, shucks, I know some saintly sorts so covered up with hair you can't tell whether they have chins or ears. I don't reckon hair has much to do with the Lord's opinion of us. If our salvation depends on hair length, then we could go to the barber shop instead of the cross and get saved. In that case, a shaved head would be the most saved amongst us.

Come to think of it, Samson did real well discomfiting the Philistines as long as his hair was long. But when devilish Delilah got him to take a nap on her lap, she had his hair cut off; and he ended up grinding in the prison house for awhile. Later, when his hair grew, he put on a performance that brought the house down (Judg. 16). Just shows that God uses all kinds of folks to get His work done.

Jesus said, "Judge not according to the appearance, but judge righteous judgment" (John 7:24).

Wouldn't it be fine if we would take time to get to know a person before we hang him with our judgment?

A Blunder and a Blessing

Mary Wiggins is a conspicuous Christian. In her eighty-plus years, many joys and much trouble have crossed her threshold. Because of her buoyant faith in Jesus, ol' man trouble has had to take a back room and let joy have the parlor.

Love is the energy which propels her. She loves good things—the Lord, church, the Bible, family, and friends.

These make her a wealthy lady, wealth on which no taxes have to be paid, eternal treasure. To top it off, she possesses a contagious sense of humor. No grumbler this one. Her laughter is often turned on herself for some blunder she has made.

One time she made a miscalculation. Turned out to bring an additional blessing to her, plus laughter to others who heard about it.

Waking up one morning, she read the clock at seven fifteen. Her day began with the usual routine of dressing, fixing breakfast, and a time of Bible reading and prayer. That always got her off to a good start.

Now I don't know if she felt a little drowsy or just sensed something was out of kilter. Anyway, when she looked the clock in the face again, it told her something. She had gotten up at twenty-five til three. Most clocks have a long hand and a short one. Her eyes had played a trick on her and the hands looked switched.

Her neighbor may have wondered at the laughter in the next apartment when folks are supposed to be asleep. But "Miss" Mary redonned her nightclothes, crawled back in bed and tried it again at eight.

Consider the blessings. She got double nourishment— two breakfasts instead of one. She hid a few extra Scriptures in her mind and had some valuable conversation with her best Friend, Jesus. Beyond doubt some of us got blessed while we slept and she prayed. Then, if she hadn't cut this caper, we wouldn't be smiling right now.

There's another whopper of a possibility that could have happened. She would've had a jump on us slumberers. Jesus said, "Be ye also ready: for in such an hour as ye think not the Son of man cometh" (Matt. 24:44). That means unexpectedly. Could well have been the time her awaited Saviour would appear.

That grand event is yet to come. Jesus said He would be back. "Watch therefore: for ye know not what hour your Lord doth come" (Matt. 24:42).

Three o'clock or eight o'clock, it doesn't matter; just so we're ready at whatever hour He appears.

9

Tall Truths from . . .
Being a Treasurer
of Tender Moments

An Elevator Temple

Dr. Charles Howard, known as pastor, preacher, teacher, and evangelist, lives in Buies Creek, North Carolina. Through this gifted man the Lord has touched many lives. His tender heart reaches out to all. In his presence, you know you are in His presence.

I heard him relate an experience in an elevator. Though going up physically, in the spiritual realm he went up, then down, then up again. The last up was joy *unspeakable.*

A stranger riding with him asked where he could get a drink. Taking advantage of a witnessing opportunity, he replied, "I don't know, but I can tell you where you can get the Water of life." This angered the man who was thirsting for spirits, not the Spirit. Dr. Howard was cursed and thought maybe the man was going to hit him. This, of course, broke the heart of this seeker of souls. Trying to go up, he found himself down—down in the valley of what he considered failure.

The angry man, who had come so close to "a well of water springing up into everlasting life" (John 4:14), left the car on which he could have gone higher than he'd ever been. And Dr. Howard stood there—dejected, crying. His opportunity to win a soul to Jesus was gone.

But was it?

The lady operating the elevator asked, "Mister, would you tell me about that Water of life?" Lo and behold, he was going up again! And God gave him the privilege of leading that dear lady "unto living fountains of water" (Rev. 7:17). An ordinary elevator car suddenly became a temple, and a thirsty soul met Jesus who said, "Whosoever drinketh of the water that I shall give him shall never thirst" (John 4:14).

I shall never forget the chills that ran over me upon hearing that story or the desire in my heart for a double portion of the Spirit who works so effectively in Charles Howard. Heaven's ranks will be swollen with those who have drunk from the cup he so graciously offers to all he meets.

The writer of Proverbs says, "He that winneth souls is wise" (11:30). And Daniel carries it higher: "They that be wise shall shine as the brightness of the firmament; and they that turn many to righteousness as the stars for ever and ever" (12:3).

Even an elevator, with someone like Charles Howard aboard, can lift a pilgrim all the way to heaven.

A Day to Remember

A sense of reverence came over me as I held a certain New Testament in my hand. The story Gideon Rollin Burhans told me made it a special Book.

Upon induction for service in World War II, a young

soldier had received this Gideon New Testament. At the time he was not a Christian. Often his wife carried him to the throne of grace on the wings of prayer—for safety and salvation.

He survived the death march of Bataan, but later died in a prison camp. Having left instructions that his personal belongings be returned to his wife, a wounded buddy finally fulfilled his request, a couple of years later. His only belonging was his New Testament.

This was no ordinary New Testament. Paying little attention to it at first, it undoubtedly became important to the soldier. In captivity, rather than have the enemy find and destroy it, he buried it several times in Bataan soil. Somehow it survived and was dug up by his friend. As touching as that is, something else made it the most important thing in the world to the young wife.

Inside the back cover were instructions on how to be saved. There was a place for the name of the one who would receive Jesus and the date of the commitment. Inscribed were this soldier's name and the date, March 6, 1942. Peace and joy filled the wife's heart, knowing that her husband was with Jesus.

Before seeing the date of salvation, my heart was moved as I listened to the story. Then as I read the date, the Spirit welled up in me. For it was during a youth revival at 23rd and Broadway Baptist Church, Louisville, Kentucky, that I surrendered my life to preach the gospel —March 6, 1942.

What a Lord we have! Thirty-nine years ago at this writing, separated by thousands of miles, in a war and in a church, God had touched two lives. To one He gave eternal life in time to escape eternal death; to another He gave a call that would last a lifetime and reach into eternity. We both could say, "Thy word is a lamp unto my feet, and a light unto my path" (Ps. 119:105).

Due to a slight bout with polio as a child, I was discharged from the Army Reserve without getting to serve. Someday I will meet my unknown "brother" in heaven. I want to thank him for going to war and dying for my freedom. And there I will meet my Savior and will thank Him for going to the cross and dying for my salvation. Together, my saved soldier friend and I will sing a song of praise to the Lord who saved us both.

Thank God for March 6, 1942!

Encouragement

Encouragement. By definition it means "to urge on." A synonym is, "to inspirit." Call it what you will, it's something everybody needs and wants. The heart thrives on it like a cow eating clover. Maybe that old cow that "jumped over the moon" was made to feel that she could do it.

My memory clings to a reaction by my dad that still stirs my heart after over forty years. He made me feel like somebody.

Visiting in the Kentucky mountains, we had a target shooting session. The mountain boys were more familiar with shootin' irons than the city slicker was. Hitting the target was as easy for them as falling off a log. My gunslinging success was about as remote as Chester's hoping to outshoot Matt Dillon.

The target was a chip of wood stuck on a fence post. When it came my turn, they most likely figured the chip was in no mortal danger. I drew a bead on the unsuspecting target and cut down on it. Well, Sir, the hills echoed the shot, and my dad fairly shouted. He leaned over excitedly, popped his hands together, and hollered, "He hit it!" The others jubilated along with him, and I felt proud. After that, I was sure I could've shot the eye out of a mosquito at forty paces.

Now the whole shootin' match had about as much impact on history as the rifle ball had on the fence post. Nobody remembered it very long—except me. On subsequent visits, I'd look at that ol' shot-up post, and remember. The post is gone now. Dad is gone. But just last year I stood in that yard and saw with the mind's eye and heard with the mind's ear. Dad didn't know what he planted in his boy's heart that day. I have a fanciful notion that even now, when some worthwhile goal is achieved, a "He hit it!" rings out from heaven's portals. It makes a fellow want to try a little harder.

Jesus was, and is, an encourager. Before He went back to heaven, His discouraged disciples went back to fishing. Their total catch for the night was zero. Morning came. Knowing their failure, Jesus said, "Cast the net on the right side of the ship, and ye shall find" (John 21:6a).

Talk about results! "They cast therefore, and now they were not able to draw it for the multitude of fishes" (v. 6b). Simon Peter got so excited he jumped into the sea and made his way to his wonderful Lord. And Jesus kept on encouraging him 'til his dying day.

When "dis" is made to disappear from discouraged by somebody who slips an "en" in its place, we get inspirited and reach for the stars.

Pass it on.

Laps of Memories

An unadulterated heart! Rare. The big word means "pure." It's most often found in a child—a heart untampered with by impure adults. You know it's there by what the little fellow says. He says what he sees, for his eyes are attached to his heart by love strings.

Now at times words are put together just right. A memory is created that's like a floating blessing that pleasures you with each passing. You wouldn't swap it for a twenty-dollar gold piece. Especially is this true when a grandparent has it tucked away.

Five-year-old Mark was enjoying his grandmother's lap, a happy place, cushioned with love. Grandma was about to get her a blessing that would include a smile. In fact the smile would give way to a good laugh.

Stroking and patting his grandmother's cheeks, Mark said, "Gran-ma-ma, you're so pretty. You're kinda old, but you're still pretty." Well Sir, she was still in her forties and would have passed for about thirty-seven-and-a-half. His calculation of age was relative. To a child all grown-ups look big and aged. It's the Methuselah complex.

Day brighteners take many forms. Being told you look good is always a ringer, makes the heart bubble. In the case at hand, I 'spect a smile prettied up that "old" face. No doubt Mark got himself a good hug.

There'll come a time when "little Mark" will be "big Mark." He won't be holdable anymore. But, somewhere, Gran-ma-ma will be recalling days of yore. A happy little face, patting hands, and a soft voice will all come back. So will the smile.

I reckon it pays to hang some happy words on folks along the way. We just might give them something to cherish when a spell of darkness catches them. If we habitually give good words, we may get some in return to help steady us when we wobble. It works that way.

It's smart to believe what Jesus says. "Give, and gifts will be given you. Good measure, pressed down, shaken together, and running over, will be poured into your lap; for whatever measure you deal out to others will be dealt to you in return" (Luke 6:38, NEB).

Words, sincerely spoken, give us a choice spot in someone's heart—even if a questionable compliment gets mixed in.

A precious memory never grows old, wilts, or fades. Properly planted, it comes up and stays as fresh as a daisy. Why not cultivate a bumper crop of the things?

Back Slapping

"A slap on the back is better than a knock on the head." Interpretation: praise accomplishes more than criticism.

Illustration. During revival at First Baptist in Hillsborough, North Carolina, Pastor Tom Denton's five-year-old son, Josh, came into the study. Having drawn a picture, he proudly showed it to his daddy.

Now daddys can react from 1 to 10 to what their offspring do. Tom must've hit 10+. He said, "Did you draw that all by yourself?" Being assured that the "Rembrandt" was his own work, Daddy Tom fairly exploded, "Fantastic!" The ear-to-ear grin on his face added heartiness. And little Josh disappeared with a singing heart.

The little fellow got slapped on the back without even being touched. Beautiful. Could be, Josh might become a famous artist someday. And, unknowingly, my friend Tom came through to this observer as a daddy who is close kin to Jesus. The good Lord knows how to lay a "well done" on those who try.

Alas, criticism comes in abundant supply and is distributed wholesale by self-employed dealers. To them, skull-cracking is more gratifying than back-patting. But it takes a fist to do one and an open palm to do the other. One hurts both; the other helps both. One makes the head hang down like Tom Dooley's; the other dekinks the spine and squares the shoulders.

Always being put down kindles ambition and confidence about as much as putting a match to a water-logged piece of firewood.

In contrast to Josh's story, I heard of a "don't" mama. Her little boy must've thought that was his middle name. No matter what he was doing, he was told "don't." One day he was real quiet. His mama hollered, "What are you doing?" He replied, "Nothing." And, in keeping with her custom, she said, "Well, stop it!" I reckon the little lad decided he couldn't even do nothing right.

Maybe the world could use a few folks like the prodigal son's father. Discouraged and smelling like a hog, the wandering boy finally came home. And his daddy said, "Bring forth the best robe, and put it on him; and put a ring on his hand, and shoes on his feet" (Luke 15:22).

It's like he was saying, "Son, you've come home. Fantastic!" I'll bet his back tingled. Like car rental folks, he most likely wanted to try harder.

There just might be some folks in reaching distance of where you are who could use a bit of praise. Figuratively speaking, hit them with a good word and watch their eyes light up like a Christmas tree. Who knows; it could even come back to you.

A Real Pickup

It was a real day brightener. I went to Durham Memorial Baptist Church to pick up my pastor friend Gerald Goodwin. He was in the kitchen of "The Land of the Little People," eating jelly biscuits and drinking coffee. Being blessed with a gentle and loving spirit, the little folk flock around him. A noisy little bunch they are, for the nice ladies have made it a happy place to be. You get the feeling that the Lord is there.

Now getting caught up in an atmosphere of love, trust, and caring is good for the heart. I found myself surrounded by a bevy of little ones, two or three years old, clamoring for attention. One reached her arms up and said, "Pick me up." I did. She grinned like a little cherub, told me her name, and I hugged her real good.

Seeing their playmate ridin' high, the others wanted to be "high and lifted up." Several took their turn. Little arms reaching up were saying, "Pay some attention to me." Then I noticed Gerald was in the pickin' up and hugging business also. We had to tear ourselves away or spend the day getting loved. We both left with singing hearts.

Several thoughts played around in my mind. First, it's as natural for a person to want to be noticed, touched, and loved as it is to eat. And age doesn't matter. "Kids" of all ages are like that. The good Lord must've made us that way.

Second, when someone bothers to pay us some attention, we respond like a hungry kitten does to a saucer of warm milk. Who can describe that "somebody cares about me" feeling? Our "responder" is always set at ready. It just needs some sensitive person to trigger it. And there's one of those lovin' gismos in every living soul.

Third, it's as possible to touch someone without getting touched as it is to shower without getting wet. As important as being held was to the little ones, the big one received more than he gave. It's just like Jesus said, "Give, and it shall be given unto you" (Luke 6:38). In short, it means give and get.

The whole "love-in" made me think of the mutual responsiveness of Jesus and little children to each other. The grown-ups thought He shouldn't be bothered with them, but He said, "[Let the] little children . . . come unto me. And he laid his hands on them" (Matt. 19:14-15). That means they touched one another and both got a blessing.

Young or old, a childlike heart can say to the Savior, "Pick me up." He's delighted to do it and no doubt smiles as He does.

The telephone company's commercial says, "Reach out, reach out and touch someone." They claim you get a lot for a little. Reaching out and touching literally turns out to be a real bargain.

10
Tall Truths from . . . Shouldering

Shouldering

Shoulders are meant for more than places to attach arms or a neck foundation. Literally and figuratively they are for resting on, crying on, and for carrying.

Shouldering is a ministry to others. Who hasn't seen a little child resting or crying on someone's shoulder or riding there?

Now a person may shed a few tears on one's own shoulder, but about all one gets in return is a wet sleeve. Sleeping on one's own shoulder earns a crick in the neck. Even a contortionist would be hard put to ride on his own shoulders. The object is to make them available to folks who need them.

Putting your head on someone's shoulder carries a bonanza. You get their arms around you, too. That's like hoping someone at least likes you and finding out they really love you. And the arms are rooted in the heart.

A husband ought to thank his lucky stars if his wife's shoulder is always available. There are times when he needs a place to cry. At other times he just needs to lay his weary head on a shoulder whose owner cares. By providing her husband a shoulder of flesh, she also provides that invisible shoulder that lifts his spirit.

Now the husband's shoulder may be bony and extra firm, but it's a fine place for a wife's head. It needs to be tear absorbent and quietening. And it needs to be there when needed. Happy is the wife whose husband's shoulders are more than a coat hanger or suspender's holders. (Note: For best results, always remove hair curlers.)

"Cold shoulder" dislocates the whole caring process. Maybe the wedding vows ought to say, "I promise to love and to cherish and to be a warm, loving shoulder." It might just prove to be that extra something that all marriages need. Could even save a few.

In telling of God's love, Jesus said it's like a shepherd who hunts for his lost sheep. "And when he hath found it, he layeth it on his shoulders, rejoicing" (Luke 15:5).

Maybe that's a picturesque way of showing us where we are when God finds us and lifts us. It's a good place to be, on God's shoulder.

And maybe He wants to use us as His shoulders on which tired, tearful folks can rest.

Christmas in the Marketplace

It happened in Thalhimers Department Store—Christmas personalized in a mother. Unaware of what she was doing, a bystander's heart was touched.

Accompanied by her little boy, Mama was shopping. Now present buying can get a little hectic—like writing a check and then remembering something else and having to write another. Like having your shopping bag fall off the counter, spilling some of the contents. There was a reasonable measure of calmness in it all, but that's not the point of this observation.

Her little boy, atop a stool and leaning on the counter, wanted mama to be an imitator—in the midst of such "important" goings on, mind you. "Be a chicken." Mama did a fine piece of clucking. "Be a horse." So she neighed. "Be a pencil." A pencil? How do you be a pencil? Wonderingly, I waited. So mama put her hands over her head, fingers touching, like the point of a pencil. The little fellow was pleased. Leaning over, she said something to him and kissed his kissable cheek.

Something more, apologizing for the delay in the second check writing, she asked the kind clerk to go ahead and take care of my purchase.

In the midst of a season of pushing, shoving, stomping, and grabbing in the name of Christmas, I saw the true spirit of Christmas. It's love. It's kindness. It's giving. It's politeness. It's responding. It's thinking of others. It's substance instead of tinsel. It's selflessness. It's acting like Jesus in honoring His birthday.

I do not know who the lady is, but unbeknownst to herself, she gave me a Christmas present that day. Without money and without price, she made me think of the One of whom it was said, "For unto you is born this day in the city of David a Saviour, which is Christ the Lord" (Luke 2:11).

My day was brightened with the star of Bethlehem, and my soul did magnify the Lord. For Christmas is Christ.

Lots of Love

Ways of saying "I love you" are as numberless as the goose bumps those words can raise. Little, unexpected acts speak louder than thunder, though expressed in cotton softness. The ol' heart jumps in delight, and the gold band that binds it to its mate glows.

I 'spose most folks have side interests along with their main occupations. Preaching is my heavenly calling, but cars are an earthly delight to me. I flat enjoy looking at 'em and swapping when possible. I've been known to do some trading that put intelligence in question.

We rode to Southern Seminary in a 1941 Chevrolet. Three years and eight cars later, we rode away in a 1939 Chevrolet. That caper included working up to a new 1950 Nash and falling back to a 1930 Model A Ford. Named that one Pepsi-Cola—"more bounce to the ounce."

Somehow my wife could neither share nor understand this love affair between man and machine. She may have felt threatened. No need, though, I love her better than the thirty cars I've had. I wouldn't swap her for a Rolls Royce. Her low-gear enthusiasm developed kinda naturally.

Now there's a humdinger of a car lot at Louisburg, North Carolina. Sets up on a knoll near the highway. Many a time I'd be bound to drive through just to see the offerings. Even knowing my wife wouldn't take too kindly to the detour, I'd do it. She'd suffer in silence. But one day she took me by surprise.

We came to the intersection across from that enticing spot. Harriett was driving. I was sure we'd head on toward home. I kept my yearnings to myself, just knowing there was no hope. Then it happened. She said, "Anything up there you want to look at?" Would a dealer like to sell a hundred cars in a day?

Now I don't recall what cars I saw or if I even looked at all. I do remember that my sweet wife was trying to please me at some cost to herself. Cars are about as exciting to her as dishwashing; but here she was, coddling my whim. Without saying it, she was saying, "I love you." Well, Sir, I fell in love with her all over again. Didn't do much for her appreciation for as fine a thing as a car, but she sure put on a fine demonstration of what love's all about. Has something to do with putting the other fellow ahead of yourself.

The Bible says, "[Love] suffereth long, and is kind . . . seeketh not her own . . . is not easily provoked . . . endureth all things . . . [and] never faileth" (1 Cor. 13:4-5, 7-8). Sounds for the world like the love of Jesus toward us weary travelers.

A little kindness does wonders for a husband and wife who never grow tired of knowing the other one cares.

Take a ride with that loving fact.

Stringless Love

It was one of those things that gives your heartstrings a real twang.

Being near Father's Day, a group of little children were asked by a news reporter why they love their daddies. The clip was shown on the TV news.

Most of the answers had to do with dads taking them places and buying them things—kind of a give-and-get relationship. Which, of course, has something to do with love, but not everything.

The star of the show appeared to be about two years old. He wasn't trying to steal the show; he was just being his honest little self. With head ducked, he said, "I wuv 'im cause if I don't wuv 'im I might get in twuble." It made you want to pick him up and hug him. It caused the grown-ups to laugh, but somehow you felt sorry for the little one. Sounded like he was afraid not to love " 'im."

I wondered, *had he been taught that to be loved depended on being good?* To him loving was obedience that brings reward. Mamas sometime say, "If you're not nice, mama won't love you." That's making loving like a water spigot to turn off or on, depending upon what kind of bucket is under it. Love is not a big stick to hold over a little head to make it do right.

Grown folks often put one another in the pressure cooker of "You love me and show it or you're in trouble." With enough of that kind of heat, the ol' lid is apt to blow off the pot sooner than later.

Husbands and wives have been known to exercise such "loving" demands on each other. It makes caressing the demander as much fun as petting a porcupine. Jesus said, "Love one another as I have loved you" (John 15:12). That's as undemanding and unselfish as a loving heart can get—no threats.

The ultimate tragedy is when the idea is attributed to God. I heard a song once, and once was enough, that mentioned things folks ought not do. Then the repetitious phrase sounded a warning in your ears, "God's gonna gitcha for that, God's gonna gitcha for that." It'd be as easy to love that kind of God as for a country crook to love the county sheriff.

Now to say that God loves our sins, or even overlooks

them, is to confess ignorance of a holy God. But to say that God loves us sinners and makes no demands of perfection on our part to receive His love is as true as Scripture. It says, "God demonstrates His own love toward us, in that while we were yet sinners, Christ died for us" (Rom. 5:8, NASB). And, "We love him because He first loved us" (1 John 4:19).

Love is not something we earn. It's a gift without strings.

Ice Capade

The fear of falling is inborn. To fall is at worst hurtful and at best embarrassing. I saw a good example of how to keep from falling.

The ice was still patchy around the post office. A daddy and his little boy, who looked to be about two, were heading for the door. Swish went the little fellow's feet, right out from under him. But he never hit the ground. One thing made the difference between safety and squalling: his daddy was holding his hand.

Now suppose the little one had been trying to hold onto his dad. He would've fallen just as sure as the fabled snowman's name is Frosty. But pop's paw was about three or four times bigger than his and stronger, like steel is stronger than string. His feet made a scrambling pattern in the air; he dangled but never dropped. As long as he was being held, he was as secure as a cub bear in his mamma's den.

Now look at the "ice capade" through spiritual specs. Many a pilgrim mistakenly thinks he must manage to hold onto the Lord if his salvation is to hold out. That'd be like sending the Rockefellers a hundred dollars so their money won't run out. Some folks won't even give the Lord a chance to save them for fear that they're not strong enough to hold on. Truth is, none of us is. Knowing this, God reaches down, takes hold of us, and we learn to say, "Thy right hand hath holden me up" (Ps. 18:35). He's the holder, we are the holdees.

Not only does He hold us secure when He saves us, but He can carry us across the slick spots in life.

Temptation to do wrong is about the slickest spot of all. It can be as alluring as a frozen pond on a moonlit night is to an ice skater. Man's fallen nature dupes him into thinking there's no danger of his falling. But his self-sufficiency usually puts the skids under him; bruising, embarrassing.

Jesus has walked across all the icy places ahead of us— "[For He] was in all points tempted like as we are, yet without sin" (Heb. 4:15). He's the only one to face temptations without falling. He knows where every slick spot is and offers to carry us over them. As long as our hand is in His, our feet can fly in forty directions; but He won't drop us. Like a general after a successful battle, we can say, "Thou hast . . . delivered my feet from falling . . . my feet did not slip" (Ps. 116:8; 18:36).

Better still, God has said, "Behold, I have graven thee upon the palms of my hands" (Isa. 49:16). That's about as much in His hands as we can be. With security like that, we can even walk across a glacier.

Burden Bearing

Unless we have suffered, we can neither understand nor enter into the suffering of others.

Job's three friends came to him in his desolation. "They sat down with him upon the ground seven days and seven nights, and none spake a word unto him: for they saw that his grief was very great" (Job 2:13). But when they finally spoke, their words were heavy and accusing. They were more eloquent in silence than in speech. Not having been devastated, how to deal with devastation was not in their handbook of "How to Help Hurting Humans."

Walking in the other traveler's moccasins is prerequisite for something other than a shallow "I'm sorry."

With all of the suffering in the world, I suppose God allows some of us to sip from the bitter cup for a purpose. The taste of it enables us to give a measure of comfort to someone who has to drink all of it.

Thirteen-year-old David Stone had an incurable sickness. Heaven's gate was ajar, and the angel was awaiting God's command to bring him home. Uneasiness about the untraveled journey filled the little boy's heart, for he knew he was going to die.

I sat by his hospital bed. He said, "I'm afraid." Having been operated on, I knew the meaning of fear. I said, "David, I was in the hospital, and I was afraid. Do you know what I did? I prayed. Would you like for us to pray?" He said, "Yes."

And so, together we talked with the Lord. The gracious Book says, "Seek ye the Lord while he may be found, call ye upon him while he is near" (Isa. 55:6). We found ourselves in His presence. The prayer ended, and David said, "I'm not afraid anymore."

And David never needed to be afraid anymore forever. In a little while he entered the place Jesus prepared where there's nothing to fear.

Of the many endearing things about Jesus, the fact that He was "a man of sorrows, and acquainted with grief" (Isa. 53:3) draws us to Him. Knowing "He hath borne our griefs, and carried our sorrows" (v. 4) makes a suffering pilgrim cry, "He's my friend; He understands!"

11

Tall Truths from . . . Listening to the Voices of Children

Unreasonable Excuses

Any excuse is good enough if you don't aim to do a thing. That's a pretty well-known piece of rhetoric and sometimes crops up in an unusual way.

Five-year-old Daniel was offered a chew of tobacco by a neighboring farmer. That's carrying neighborliness a mite far, but the little kid accepted his offer. He cut down on it and found out it didn't come close to chocolate candy. The wad needed to be disposed of in short order. When he spit it out, his aim fell short. His socks suddenly turned a streaky brown.

Later, some other bighearted soul said, "Daniel, do you want a chew of tobacco?" Instead of saying he didn't like it or didn't want any, seems he figured he needed a reason for refusing. So it came out, "Naw, I get it on my socks."

Now, for a bystander, without the facts, that must've sounded like a strange reply. About as strange as a lazy farmer saying he won't plant a crop because it might rain on it. Just like there are times when we all cover up our real reasons for not doing something.

Daniel didn't miss a thing by disguising his sure-nuff reason for not taking another chew. But in the spiritual arena, a person can miss a lot.

Jesus tells a mind-grabbing story illustrating the disaster of not accepting an invitation to have a seat in the kingdom of God (Luke 14:16-24).

A host of folks were invited to a sumptuous meal. Three of the invitees sent word to the inviter that, for various reasons (?), they would have to decline. One bought some land and was bound to go look at it. One bought some oxen and had to prove them. One got married and had to stay home. And so one was earthbound, one proved himself dumber than an ox, and the other may have been henpecked. Not a one gave the truth about not accepting the gracious invitation; the truth being the supper wasn't important to them. They didn't want to go.

Many a person has felt the tug of God's Spirit in his heart, inviting him to become a part of His church. Excuses for not accepting are as varied as the colors in Joseph's coat and as sensible as a beggar turning down an invitation to eat at the Waldorf-Astoria.

One says he was forced to go to church as a child. Another complains of the hypocrites in the church. Still another is too busy and another too tired. These are cover-ups for saying, "I don't need it, I don't want it, and I'll not do it."

Jesus said of such, "None of those men which were bidden shall taste of my supper" (Luke 14:24).

When the Lord invites us to come to Him, excuses, true or false, can be right dangerous things.

Careful, now. Don't spit on your socks.

The Bible Is for Believing

Children have a way of accepting the Bible at face value. When Jesus says, "I stand at the door, and knock: if any man hear my voice, and open the door, I will come in" (Rev. 3:20), a child is apt to believe it. He has heard about Jesus coming into your heart and most likely pictures a door through which He enters.

Five-year-old Brian Woodell was sure that Jesus literally comes to live in the heart. He had a serious concern about his granddaddy and about Jesus.

Granddad, an ex-smoker, was carrying Brian toward the house. Being kinda short-winded, he had to set his little treasure down for a rest. Brian's curiosity being aroused, he raised a straightforward question: "Granddaddy, have you started smoking again?" The answer was, "No." Relieved, Brian said, "I sure am glad. Smoking turns your heart black inside. And when Jesus comes into your heart, His face will get all black." He rubbed his little hand all over his own face to emphasize the seriousness of the matter.

I have a notion that Jesus took note that day of a little boy's concern for Him. And down time's corridor echoed His gracious words, "[Let the] little children . . . come unto me: for of such is the kingdom of heaven" (Matt. 19:14). I reckon the Master's great heart is made glad by those who simply love Him and believe Him.

Most folks know that there are poetic and figurative words in the Bible. Then there are others that are just as plain as the nose on your face. Jesus referred to Himself as the Vine, Bread, Water, Light, the Door, Shepherd, and more. These have to be interpreted. But when He says, "He that heareth my word, and believeth on him that sent me, hath everlasting life, and shall not come into condemnation; but is passed from death unto life" (John 5:24), it's best to take Him literally and get on with believing.

Sin makes the heart dirty. And a dirty heart is a heavy thing to carry around. For our sins, Jesus got His face dirty on the cross with sweat, blood, and tears. When He is invited to come into a man's heart, He makes it new and clean.

Brian's Jesus said, "Blessed are the pure in heart: for they shall see God" (Matt. 5:8).

And you can believe it!

The Lost and the Found

The word *lost* means something out of place. It applies to those who are not in Christ; it can also apply to Christians not living in God's will. Both are serious.

Three-year-old granddaughter Valerie was visiting us. Those times are as enjoyable as a banana split, but occasionally you feel you've had enough for a little while. That "I've got to get away for a few minutes" sensation grabs you. Every grandparent can identify with that.

Needing a little peace and quiet, I slipped outdoors to soak up the cool darkness. I neither wanted to talk nor be talked to. My ears had that cluttered feeling.

Valerie had seen my exit and started calling, "Papa Jones! Papa Jones!" Her little voice is music to my heart, but at the moment I could do without the sound of music. The night had swallowed me up, so her pleading call was answered with silence. When there was no answer, she turned and said with astonishment to those in the house, "He has LOST his self!"

Now I wasn't really lost, but I wasn't where my grand-baby wanted me to be. So, in a sense, I was lost.

Pondering the experience, I found a truth. Even God's people can be where He doesn't want us to be. A man can deliberately choose the way of darkness and lose "his self." He gets in the dark, and gradually the dark gets into him. He misses all those good things God had planned for him over in the light. It makes as much sense as walking down an unfamiliar road on a stormy night and blowing out the lantern.

Sometimes folks get "lost" by wandering. Nothing deliberate, but separation results. Son Mark was about five. We got separated in a big store, causing that panicky feeling. Presently the loudspeaker blared, "We've got a little boy here in a gray overcoat who says his daddy's lost." We belonged together but too much distance had gotten between us.

It's possible for us to be attracted by the world's tinsel and lose sight of our Heavenly Father and find ourselves lost to His protective care. But He always comes looking for us. That's His way.

Jesus said, "Men loved darkness rather than light, be-cause their deeds were evil" (John 3:19). That's being lost. But to the "found," Jesus says, "I am the light of the world: he that followeth me shall not walk in darkness, but shall have the light of life" (John 8:12). That's being saved.

Why wander aimlessly in the dark, when, as the song says, "How beautiful to walk in the steps of the Saviour, led in paths of light"?

Fencing in Our Wants

"In those days there was no king in Israel: every man did that which was right in his own eyes" (Judg. 21:25). Sounds like everybody danced to his own tune. It's much like today's attitude. Even with rulers and laws aplenty, most folks are singing "don't fence me in."

Four-year-old Daniel Hopkins supplied an illustration of how the "do-what-you-like" syndrome works.

The little lad kissed a little lass at nursery school. He either kissed and told or was told on. His mama heard about it and felt impelled to do some inquiring. After all, kissing at four is right heady stuff.

"Where did you kiss her, Daniel?" said concerned mama. "On the playground," said honest Daniel. Now mama was thinking about anatomy instead of geography, so she redirected the inquisition. "No, I mean where on the face did you kiss her?" His answer reflected innocent candor: "On the lips." As much as to say, "Where else?"

Suddenly the thing was more serious than first suspected. A natural question had to be raised. "Why did you do that?" With no hesitation, the pint-sized Don Juan answered, "Because we both wanted to."

To smooch or not to smooch; that is not the question. The point of this minor league soap opera is that a thing is not necessarily right just because a person wants to do it. His "wanter" may be about as trustworthy as a switched crossroads sign. We need help in sorting out right from wrong. Without a "king" to rule over our desires, our wants may become wantonness.

The conversation of a couple of Christian young men was overheard. One said, "I drink all the liquor I want, and I curse all I want to." Had it ended there, Christianity would be as appealing to some folks as a phony C-note is to a counterfeiter. But when he added, "I just don't want to," I was as relieved as a heartburn that met up with an antacid. He had King Jesus on the throne of his wants.

David let his unruled desires play havoc with him a time or two. He learned better when he discovered God's ways are always right. Then he said, "I delight to do thy will, O my God: yea, thy law is within my heart" (Ps. 40:8).

Wanting to please the Lord elevates our wants like a bridge over an infested swamp. It's good to have God's approval on a thing before we embrace it.

Aspire to Be a Rock

Nine-year-old Mark Hopkins was in a children's musical. His portrayal of a talking spider was as finely done as a spun web. Included in the scenery were papier-mache rocks which looked real and substantial, being good hiding places for scurrying spiders.

Seven-year-old brother Daniel took it all in from his front-row vantage point. The whole thing made a deep impression on him and aroused a desire to be in the cast.

After the grand finale, his longings were verbalized. Said he to his proud-as-punch-mom, "I wish I could've been in it." Wondering about the pint-sized would-be-actor's aspirations, she said, "What would you have wanted to be?" "A rock," was his solid reply. Next question: "Why would you want to be a rock?" Answer: "I didn't want to say anything: I just wanted to be in it."

I reckon a talking rock would be as likely as a talking

spider, but Daniel preferred emoting to line saying. He just wanted to have a part in what was going on.

Now rocks are important. They make fine foundations, serve as roadbeds, help hold the world together, come in various shapes and colors, and often are real valuable. God knew what He was doing when He created rocks. They never say anything, they just mutely do their job. They are indispensable.

Figuratively, God is described as a Rock. What a dependable picture! Unlike rocky rocks, God sometimes speaks. But, whether silent or audible, He's that indestructable Being upon which we can safely stand or behind which we find shelter.

The psalmist identified the God upon whom his soul waited: "He only is my rock and my salvation; he is my defence" (62:2). In stress, he said, "When my heart is overwhelmed, lead me to the rock that is higher than I" (61:2). And Christ is identified as the spiritual Rock that followed ancient Israel: "For they drank of that spiritual Rock that followed them: and that Rock was Christ" (1 Cor. 10:4). The trusting heart cries, "On Christ the solid rock I stand!"

Jesus gave Simon a new name—Peter. It means stone or rock. He then said, "Upon this rock I will build my church" (Matt. 16:18). And all who become part of His church become building rocks. "Lively stones," we are called (1 Pet. 2:5).

There are many necessary "talking rocks" in the church. But the Lord has multitudes of faithful doers who don't say much. They, too, honestly "want to be in it." Their faith is unbreakable, their loyalty is unmovable, they are as dependable as the rising sun. Without these relatively quiet rocks, the church would crumble like an imploded building. They attend, they pray, they give, they love, they live the gospel, they give cups of cold water in the Savior's name.

Jesus never said we have to be eloquent in speech to be in life's most important drama. Silence can be eloquent when it comes from a rock who is in "The Rock."

Looking at Jesus and His wonderful church, the wise person says, "I wish I could be in it." Jesus says, "What do you want to be?" Reverently he says, "A rock." And through repentance and faith, He makes him one. Joyfully, he discovers a rock is a fine thing to be.

It would appear that anyone who does not want to be in the church that "Christ . . . loved . . . and gave himself for" (Eph. 5:25) might have rocks in his head.

Celestial Sunbathing

Near the end of the Bible these solemn words are recorded: "For I testify unto every man that heareth the words of the prophecy of this book, If any man shall add unto these things, God shall add unto him the plagues that are written in this book" (Rev. 22:18). That's enough warning to make a man be careful about how he handles God's Word. I calculate as how such a stringent statement wouldn't apply to Valerie, our three-year-old granddaughter.

Once upon a visit, the little thing came into my study. Didn't add much to sermon preparation, but add something she did. Her "something" will be remembered when whatever profound pronouncements I was preparing have played out. Climbing up on my lap, she wanted me to read some Bible verses and let her repeat them after me. You've never heard such translations! Seemed to satisfy her little heart. Papa Jones's heart sang a tune.

Her next visit called for another session of "Bible study." Only this time she wanted to "read," and I was to repeat. Perched on my lap, she opened the Bible. Some of the "verses" came close to what the Bible says, some were pretty farfetched. "The Lord is a very good Lord." That one echoed like a psalm. The next one was "found" several pages away. "God lays out in the sun." That's about as near to Holy Writ as a church steeple is to a church basement. But coming from a deep place in a little girl's guileless heart gave it an authentic ring. It was almost impossible to repeat that one with a straight face.

Jesus said concerning the little ones, "In heaven their angels do always behold the face of my Father which is in heaven" (Matt. 18:10). I wouldn't be surprised if the reporting angel didn't create quite a stir in heaven with that one.

Maybe Valerie figured if God made the sun He could lie out in it if He wanted to. She knew folks can do it so why not God? No need to rationalize though. It was a nice warm thought about God who is as real to her as her nighttime security blanket.

Big folks need to be cautious about making the Bible say something it doesn't say. Little children have the privilege of seeing the Lord and His Word with the heart. Jesus said, "Except ye be converted; and become as little children, ye shall not enter the kingdom of heaven" (Matt. 18:3). Must mean it takes a childlike, believing heart to get in.

Look beyond God's sun and you see God's Son.

12

Tall Truths from . . .
Being a Caretaker
of the Family

Family 'Cycle

Family—a beautiful concept, launched from the heart of God. A husband, a wife, and some children conjure up the image. A certain family caught my attention when I yielded the traffic right-of-way to them. Their mode of transportation spoke to my heart and set off a chain of thoughts that wheeled into my mind.

A bicycle built for two had become one built for four. Mama, up front, had a little tyke strapped in a basket in front of her. Daddy, on the rear seat, had a baby attached to his back, papoose style. The wind-whipped smile on the little one's face said he was having the ride of his life. And I smiled to myself in sheer enjoyment at the sight.

What a picture of scriptural truths about family! They were pulling together, heading toward the same goal, and enjoying the journey. That must be what God had in mind when He peopled the earth with families.

Other reflections got to pedaling around in my head. Dad had put mom ahead of himself where he could watch out for her and protect her. Mom was in a position to see things he might not see and to give guidance. Moms are like that. The children were included in what the family was doing and they were secure. Harmony and rhythm said, "This family's together."

A few more comparisons coasted along. They had to agree on the route and be mindful of ever-present dangers—like potholes and traffic. Keeping their balance under pressure was a must. Leaning in opposite directions would wreck them.

Now a wise family invites Jesus to ride with them on the vehicle of God's love. Getting where they ought to go is more sure that way. There'll be some "potholes" en route, but the Bible shows how to steer around them. If one is run into, there's no need to let it jar the life out of the family. Get up and move along. And the Lord knows how to keep us out of wrong "traffic."

Families can have a fine scenic ride traveling God's way. The order is this: "As the church is subject unto Christ, so let the wives be unto their own husbands in every thing. Husbands, love your wives, even as Christ also loved the church, and gave Himself for it. Children, obey your parents in the Lord: for this is right" (Eph. 5:24-25; 6:1).

The "bicycle family" was wheeling and dealing. The wheeling was obvious; the dealing out of a lovely picture was done unconsciously. I'm glad I was there when they passed by.

Pedal with Jesus on earth, and you'll ride right through the gates of glory.

A Tale of Two Families

Enough is enough. This truth was expressed in a most unexpected way in a most unlikely place.

When our son Mark was about seven, he sometimes swept the floor at Gene Pearce's barber shop in Rolesville. Made himself a piece of change that way. Once his mind must've been on the family more than on his job.

To all in the shop he had a right revealing statement to make. To this day, no one knows why. In his boyish drawl, he said, "Cathy was born in Louisville, Hannah was born in Rockingham, I was born in Asheboro, and Russell was born in Rolesville. Every time we move Mama has another baby. Mama said she don't want to move anymore." Well, sir, the patrons had a hard time squelching their laughter. He wasn't trying to be funny. The little kid wasn't kidding that mama didn't want any more kids. Turned out that four were enough. Each being worth a million dollars, we figured we were about as wealthy as we could afford to be.

The psalmist said, "Children are an heritage of the Lord. . . . As arrows are in the hand of a mighty man; so are children of the youth. Happy is the man that hath his quiver full of them" (127:3-5). Our "quiver" was full aplenty with the little "arrows" from the Lord's bow. They brought happiness, too.

Our family was small compared to Harriett's grandmother's. She birthed fifteen and raised eleven of them. When she was about ninety, Harriett's daddy said, "Mammy, one thing sure; having children won't kill you, will it?" In all seriousness, she said, "I don't know, Congleton, I'm in pretty bad shape." The dear soul entered the pearly gates at ninety-three. Childbearing finally took its toll.

Now the number of children in a family is not the important thing. It's whether each one gets the chance to be "born again." That's critical. The naturally born wear out. The spiritually born live forever. The sweetest thing this side of heaven is a Christian family.

The jailer asked Paul how to be saved. He was answered, "Believe on the Lord Jesus Christ, and thou shalt be saved, and thy house" (Acts 16:31). They did and they were. That way, when the family circle down here is broken, it will be reformed "over there." Then the circle will be unbroken—forever.

Don't kid the kids about Jesus.

Heaven Came Down

It was the last night we would spend at the home place with my wife's mother. The time had come for her to move to the Baptist Home for her remaining years. Breaking up home is sad. It's a time of looking back and knowing things will never be the same. You want to gather within your mind all you can and store in your heart those treasures that will last a lifetime. It's an emotional journey.

God never created a more beautiful night. It was studded with twinkling stars, "bright as diamonds in the sky," shining against the deep blue overhead canopy. The countryside was peaceful and quiet—except for the night sounds echoing from the woods.

Near the back side of the house stands an aged, weather-tested walnut tree. It has withstood severe storms, blistering sun, and freezing cold. It has been lightning struck, riddled in target shooting, and been home for birds, squirrels, and insects. Yet, through it all, it grew strong, tall, and productive. It reminded me of the family to which it gave its shade.

I stood, gazing heavenward through gnarled limbs that looked like arms reaching for the stars. And the dazzling stars were as brilliant Christmas tree lights hanging on the old tree's branches. What a magnificent sight.

Like being caught up in a never-to-be-forgotten experience, awesomeness and reverence filled my soul. God's presence intermingled with the nocturnal beauty and the soul's longings.

My thoughts reached back thirty-four years. Pleasant, happy memories cascaded across my mind like a melodious waterfall. Bits and pieces of melancholy surfaced and then flowed on. The joys and tears of so many years were compacted together for review. It was a hallowed moment.

The Bible says, "The heavens declare the glory of God" (Ps. 19:1). 'Tis true. His glory shown 'round about me. The only proper position before Him was on my knees—there in the place where we had met many times before. I cried over remembered failures and unfulfilled dreams, praised Him for His infinite blessings, and made an honest attempt toward a fuller commitment to Jesus Christ. Like Jacob, I could say, "Surely the Lord is in this place. . . . This is none other but the house of God, and this is the gate of heaven" (Gen. 28:16-17).

Somehow the "last night" became like the last chapter in a "to-be-continued" story. The final ending will gather all the parts into a whole that makes sense.

The place that Jesus has gone to prepare is a place of understanding life's mysteries, reunion, the wiping away

of all tears, and completeness. Old home places give way to the many mansions in the Father's house (John 14:2).
Hallelujah!

Old Trunks and Resurrection

The beautiful Horsman doll was dearly loved by my wife as a child. But children grow up and dolls are put away, only to live in memories of bygone, happy childhood days.

For many years the doll had slept in the old trunk upstairs at the home place. A trunk filled with treasures bridging today with countless yesterdays.

The time comes when home places have to be broken up and folks have to move on. Such a time had arrived. Harriett asked me to find her doll. Raising the trunk lid and lifting out the tray, I saw her lying there, a shadow of her former beautiful self. Time had taken its toll. She had on no dress, her arms and legs were pitted, her cloth body had been patched, she had had an operation for the removal of her crier, and her eyes were closed.

As though touching something special, I gently picked her up. I loved her because she was a part of the wife I love. Then something happened. The moment I held her in an upright position, those long-closed eyes popped open. It was as if she had come back to life. And she looked happy.

Taking her downstairs, Harriett held her as she used to. I could almost see the thoughts that must have filled her mind. She plans to have the doll restored and someday give her to a granddaughter. It will be something old, lovingly made new to become a part of another life.

As the "Drama of the Doll" unfolded, I saw a picture of the experience of Christians. We live out our days on earth, and, by the hands of others, are put away somewhere. It's the way things are supposed to be. Though out of sight, we live in the hearts of those who loved us. And God remembers.

On an appointed day, Jesus is to return. Old "trunks" will open everywhere. "For the Lord himself shall descend from heaven with a shout, with the voice of the archangel, and with the trump of God: and the dead in Christ shall rise first" (1 Thess. 4:16). We shall be changed, our new eyes will open, and we will see Jesus. "It is sown a natural body; it is raised a spiritual body" (1 Cor. 15:44). God will lovingly hold us in His arms, and we shall be "clothed upon, that mortality might be swallowed up of life" (2 Cor. 5:4).

What a day, what a day! What a glorious day when "death is swallowed up in victory"! (1 Cor. 15:54).

Hallelujah! There is a resurrection!

Afterthought:
Scattered Patches of Light

On Being Adopted

Adoption means a whole new kind of life for the adopted. A child, in circumstances not of his own making, is chosen by someone to become legally his. A new name is given and responsibility is assumed. It often turns out to be a happy situation. Sometimes an offer is made that has to be rejected.

Upon the death of my mother, I remarked to a young preacher's wife, "My dad died twenty-three years ago and now my mother. This is the first time in my life that I've been an orphan. I'm a fifty-nine-year-old orphan." Must've touched her heartstrings, for she quickly responded, "I'll adopt you."

Now that seemed like a real fine offer to me, especially since she was young and attractive. I shared the good news with my wife, Harriett. Quicker than a glint can come into the eye, and with put-your-foot-down finality, she blurted out, "She'd better keep her cotton-pickin' hands off of you." She settled the matter like an irreversible court decision.

Even though such adoption procedures would be unlikely, I knew my sweet wife was saying, "You're mine and nobody can have you." I may not be much but I'm all she's got in the way of a husband. Made me feel as loved, wanted, and secure as a wrinkled two-dollar bill in a miser's wallet.

The whole world is teeming with spiritual Orphan Annies in need of a Daddy Warbucks. That's a figurative way of saying they need to be received into the family of God. And everybody is an "Annie" until one is chosen and adopted. The Bible says, "God sent forth his Son . . . to redeem them that were under the law, that we might receive the adoption of sons" (Gal. 4:4-5). To those who respond, He declares, "Ye have received the Spirit of adoption, whereby we cry, Abba, Father" (Rom. 8:15).

Becoming one of God's children is like going from rags to riches. It's knowing that we belong to Someone who will never abandon us on the world's doorstep.

When the devil tries to get his orphan-making hands on Christians, Jesus says, "I give unto them eternal life; and they shall never perish, neither shall any man pluck them out of my hand" (John 10:28). In the vernacular, He might say, "Deceiver, they are mine; and you'd better keep your rotten, trickin' hands off of them!"

The adoption papers were signed in blood on the cross. There's room on them for the names of all who yearn to call God, Father.

A Flying Lesson

Among other accomplishments, Stuart Henderson is a jim-dandy pilot. He took me up for a bird's-eye view of Durham and its environs.

Now I am as apt to get airsick as a plane is to fly. On

steep left and right turns, my stomach goes in the opposite direction. Upon learning this, for both our sakes, Stuart respected my queasiness. Such stunts as loops and snap rolls were mercifully avoided altogether.

Since I had flown a Piper Club over thirty-five years ago, "Ace" let me take the controls. It was comforting to know his skilled hands were always in the ready position.

Time has a way of making familiar things unfamiliar. Unintentionally, in about five minutes, we had climbed a thousand feet. I reckon it's a preacher's natural inclination to go heavenward. Since it wasn't time to "go," we leveled off.

Since I'm not eagle-eyed, my knowledgeable friend in the front seat interpreted the scene below through the intercom. I saw the church, my home, and other important places from a higher perspective.

My sense of direction wasn't exactly like the swallows heading for Capistrano. Stuart has homing-pigeon instincts, so getting lost was as unlikely as a martin missing his gourd. Being in the hands of someone who knows the way evaporates fear like mist in the sunshine.

Time came to head for home. I knew where home was about as much as the plane did. But my guide knew. No need to fret, for I was in better hands than Allstate's.

Now landing is tricky and not meant for inexperienced hands. The strip was about country-road wide and up a slight grade. The "flying master" set us down like he had done it hundreds of times, and we taxied to a safe stop. Mission accomplished, home.

The whole thing caused some heavenly thoughts to fly through my mind. It's kinda like getting saved.

Jesus invites us to enter His plane of salvation, fastening us in securely. He carries us to previously unknown heights, from which we see things differently. Spiritual queasiness gives way to anticipation. He communicates with us, teaching us new things. His hand is always ready to correct our course, when we stray. We are not afraid, for He said, "Lo, I am with you alway" (Matt. 28:20). (When flying, He may well say, "High, I am with you, too.) And He enables us to avoid the stunts of the "prince of the air"—Satan.

The ultimate destination, heaven, is known to Jesus. A perfect landing is made on the straight and narrow runway. Upon arrival, the Father says, "Welcome home."

Like wings, salvation's description lifts. "Your life is hid with Christ in God. When Christ, who is our life, shall appear, then ye shall also appear with him in glory" (Col. 3:3-4).

And that's the plane truth.

Mice and Men

For a mouse, his gnawing noise level in the closet was high enough to awaken us. Knowing the little fellow needed nourishment, I fixed him some. A trap was baited with temptation, but next morning the cheese was gone. So was the mouse. The unsprung trap looked disappointed. Color the mouse lucky.

Rebaited, the trap was again put in place. Later I was summoned from yon side of the house by a right frightening screech that included my name. My unsuspecting wife had stepped on the trap. Fortunately her tootsies were shod, but her life span may have shrunk.

Now a trap doesn't care what it catches just so it catches

something. A varmint or a toe will do. It just naturally looks happier with a thing in its hungry mouth.

If a mouse can reason, he probably figured he outsmarted the trap. May have shared his technique with a friend. But even a preacher should be a tad brighter than a rodent, so war was declared. No such critter was going to make a fool out of me.

The kitchen being a better gleaning place, trusty trap was placed there, loaded and ready. During the night the unwanted intruder stupidly tried his luck again. And Mr. Trap snarled, "Gotcha!"

There's another kind of trap setting done by crafty old Satan. He seldom makes direct approaches; he sets traps. Wearing disguises, he's hard to recognize; for hiding his true identity is part of the trap. He never says, "Let's go sin," but, "Let's have us a ball." Sounds good.

Being smarter than we are, the devil baits the trap with our favorite temptation, makes it pretty, and always appeals to some weakness we have. The Bible says, "The lust of the flesh, and the lust of the eyes, and the pride of life, is not of the Father, but is of the world" (1 John 2:16). Wrong, strong desires are met with magnetized bait that pulls like gravity.

Sometimes we bait-nibble without getting detectably caught. Get caught just a little anyhow. It doesn't show, yet. Old Scratch plays the waiting game, and he's impartial.

Man's intelligence is never more questionable than when he tries to outsmart Satan. There comes a time when the bait has done its work and a sinister voice says, "Gotcha!"

"Resist the devil, and he will flee from you. Draw nigh to God, and he will draw nigh to you" (Jas. 4:7-8). That's a trap neutralizer.

Man may be just "a little lower than the angels" (Ps. 8:5) but sometimes he's not much higher than a mouse.

Something's Following You

Four-year-old Daniel's face was bruised noticeably, which created some curiosity. His explanation was unusual but graphic. "I was trying to get away from the ball, but it followed me."

There are hurtful "balls" in life that are thrown at us or knocked toward us from which we need to flee. They come in assorted shapes and sizes. At times they come slowly, allowing time to get out of the way. Often, they come with enough zing to zap us.

Now the "balls" that bruise are from the devil's ball bag. They are always foul and curved, never going where we think they will. If hit by one, considerable damage results.

Hophni and Phinehas, a couple of rather obscure Old Testament priests, illustrate the point (1 Sam. 2-4). Evil followed them like a cat follows the scent of mackerel. Rebelliousness, greediness, and sensuousness chased them and hit them full force. They liked it. The devil chunked them some right "base" balls.

Papa priest, Eli, made about as much attempt at curbing their sinfulness as trying to control wild mustangs with twine. The biography reads, "His sons made themselves vile, and he restrained them not" (1 Sam. 3:13). Unrestrained vileness not only bruised them black and blue, it got them killed.

It's right serious to play ball in the devil's park. His throwing arm is accurate. He will also bat a thousand against us, if he can. His efforts will continue 'till life's last inning. When one of his balls heads in our direction, it's best to "run like the devil" in the opposite direction.

The Bible tells us what to do when we're about to be beaned by a devil ball. "Put on the whole armour of God, that ye may be able to stand against the wiles of the devil . . . taking the shield of faith. . . . And take the helmet of salvation" (Eph. 6:11,16-17). That's good protection for our vulnerable noggins.

In contrast, the Lord has some beautiful "balls" which He tosses toward us. No need to run from them. Goodness and mercy are two. David, who knew the Lord as his Shepherd, said, "Surely goodness and mercy shall follow me all the days of my life" (Ps. 23:6). If we know Him, they follow us, too. That's what we get for running toward the Lord instead of away from Him.

The devil is a bruiser. God is a blesser.

Floods and Arks

Noah had his flood, and we had ours in Louisville, Kentucky, in 1937. Ours didn't cover the earth, but it sure played havoc with our end of town. Our "ark" was a tobacco warehouse. We fared better than Noah's neighbors, for a whole bunch of us went in before it was too late. Got to be real neighborly before the sewers finally swallowed that renegade Ohio River.

Curious things happen when folks are locked together in bad times. I wasn't but fourteen, but I recollect seeing different characteristics of folks come out of hiding.

We had a courtin' couple who wanted to whisper

"sweet nothings" out of earshot. That's not easy in a room half a block big and full of eyes and ears. I pestered them. My first name was Ob and my middle one was Noxious. They took it as long as they could, and then gave me a nickel to get lost. Like Satan, I left them "for a season." I turned a profit through aggravation.

Another streak of human nature got noticeable at eatin' time. The "Good Samaritans" brought us soup in big garbage cans. New ones. We'd get in line with whatever container we had. One man had a gallon tomato can. Guess he figured on getting more than the rest of us. He got a foolin'. Everybody got the same ration—a dipper full. Hope I'm wrong, but his actions made him suspect of selfishness.

While the river was still climbing, religion got high priority. Bibles were read, folks prayed, and services were held. Came a time, though, when Mr. Ohio crested and began to abate. Religious fervor seemed to abate, too, and a sizable amount of it went down the drain. The good Lord said, "He shall call upon me, and I will answer him: I will be with him in trouble; I will deliver him" (Ps. 91:15), but He likes to be called on when trouble is hiding. Emergency religion is kinda unfair to the Lord.

I saw a lady across the street trying to sweep the water off her porch as it lapped like menacing wet tongues. A broom was no match for the mighty river. Helplessness took over and a boat was sent. Comes a time when we all get dependent and have to cry for mercy.

A flood of trouble can flood our souls with a sense of need for God. Happy are we if we "come boldly unto the throne of grace, that we may obtain mercy, and find grace to help in time of need" (Heb. 4:16).

The only "ark" of safety is Jesus. If we're in Him, God

can do some perfecting work in us as we ride the floods of life. All other "arks" leak.

Truth About Lies

"I'll lie to you at the drop of a hat." That's what I overheard a man say to a fellow worker. At least he was truthful enough to admit he was a liar. I 'spect he'd lie even without a hat being dropped. When you've already dropped your character, there's no need to dirty up an innocent hat. He most likely meant he was quick on the draw when he felt a lie would suit his purpose better'n the truth.

Now it's a sad commentary on the condition of the human heart that lying has become downright respectable. We even have size and color charts by which to judge lies. Like the three bears, there are big, medium, and little lies. They range in color from black to gray to white. Some are promulgated as being harmless. Funny thing, though, the Bible knows no such foolishness. These lying claims about lies are about as truthful as saying the Grand Canyon is shallow, a lump of coal is baby blue or a rabid raccoon is a nice pet.

The art of lying has been around a long time. Cain denied knowing the whereabouts of his brother Abel whom he'd killed and buried. Ananias and Sapphira, a couple of New Testament dandies, sold their property and told a bald-faced lie about the proceeds (Acts 5:1-11). The practice hasn't let up from those days until now. Looks like it will last for time's duration.

With the omnipresence of lying, there must be a source.

And it must have power to reach all over everywhere like the sky. Jesus told the truth about it in His answer to a bunch of untruthful critics. They accused Him of lying, said He had a devil in Him and aimed to chunk some rocks at Him. What He said got them riled up. He even told them who they were kin to. "Ye are of your father the devil . . . . When he speaketh a lie, he speaketh of his own: for he is a liar, and the father of it" (John 8:44).

According to the Word, folks who lie are declaring that they are younguns of the big daddy of all lies. A family tree like that ought to cause red-faced shame.

Lie-telling on earth is as destructive as wild fire. But something more terrible waits "out yonder." "All liars shall have their part in the lake which burneth with fire and brimstone: which is the second death" (Rev. 21:8). Just think how it'd be to spend eternity where not one iota of truth could be found!

The cross of Jesus has the power to cross out the evil in a man's heart. Even an old liar can become someone you can trust—'cause he won't be a liar anymore, when Jesus, the Truth, enters him.

And that's the truth about lying!

Spuds and Jesus

Some things have to be dug for or else we do without them; like gold, potatoes, and truth.

Lonnie Weathers was a genial businessman, farmer, and friend. He had a refreshing sense of humor and loved a good give-and-take session. One day he said, "Preacher, do you want some potatoes?" I said, "Yes, Sir, I'll take some." Kind of a sensible answer to his generous offer, I thought. But he wasn't finished. "If you want 'em, you'll have to dig 'em. I'm not gonna dig 'em for you."

Now even a preacher can dig spuds, but his reply hit me broadside. A right smart answer popped into my head, so I countered with my best shot to even the score. "Why not? I dig your sermons for you." Well, sir, he dug me some potatoes and got himself a big kick out of the deal. He told somebody, "If that preacher's got that much Irish in him, I'll dig him some potatoes." Must've been Irish potatoes. I enjoyed 'em, and our friendship deepened.

Now nobody can dig truth for us. To possess it, we have to search for it. Jesus said, "The kingdom of heaven is like unto treasure hid in a field" (Matt. 13:44). Implied is that it takes digging to find it. When found, joy follows; for a man has enriched himself with value. Finding the reality of God's kingdom is like that.

Gold nuggets of truth are hidden all through the Bible. The casual reader gathers the ones on the surface. The serious "miner" will dig carefully and patiently for the "mother lode." He's never content with the little dab he gets from the pulpit. That's somebody else's diggins. To become personal treasure, truth has to be searched for and found for oneself.

Then again, going deep enough is important. There's a well at my wife's home place of some of the tastiest water ever to wet a palate. Only trouble, it used to get too low in the summertime for the pump to get it to the house. Water had to be bucket drawn and toted. Finally, somebody dug it six feet deeper through the rock and never again did it fail. It made the folks wish they'd done it years sooner.

Many a man might be just a little ways from making the grandest find of all—Jesus. Digging through the rocks of sin in his heart and the rocks of unbelief in his head, he's sure to find the Lord who's been near all the while. "The Lord is nigh unto all them that call upon him, to all that call upon him in truth" (Ps. 145:18).

Spuds and the Savior—one for the body, one for the soul. Both are available, if we dig for them.

Endurance Tested

One day my favorite pocket-size New Testament was missing. Being a gift from my wife made it special and a near constant companion. God's Word is high quality, and so was this copy. As things turned out, I'm glad it was.

Upon returning home later that day, good news greeted me. "Found your Bible," Harriett said. Glad and relieved, the obvious question was asked: "Where?" Have you ever had cold water thrown on your happiness? Her answer did it: "In the washing machine." My spirits were dampened considerably.

Now the Word of the Lord puts cleanness in a man's soul, but the Word itself has no need of a washing. It speaks of baptism, and, through my negligence, got baptized.

Instead of emptying my shirt pocket at night, I usually chunk shirt, pocket and all contents on the sofa in the bedroom. Knowing this untidy habit of mine, my wife usually checks the pocket before laundry time. She forgot. So I had the cleanest New Testament in town.

The sight of my treasure gave me that washed-out feeling. God's Word had been drenched in darkness and spun dizzy. The leather binding had separated from the soggy, but still intact pages. Passing through such a storm was enough to make it come all to pieces, but in this case it didn't. Though hurt, it survived. After several days of drying out, it was glued back in its binding and returned to service.

The wavy pages make it a thicker Testament, but not a word is missing or marred. It says exactly what it said before its terrible ordeal, offering comfort and hope. Though subjected to destructive punishment, it reaches out in love to those hungry for its message. And I cherish it more since I almost lost it.

What happened to the Book verifies this eternal truth, "The word of the Lord endureth forever" (1 Pet. 1:25). Jesus said, "Heaven and earth shall pass away, but my words shall not pass away" (Matt. 24:35). No matter what indignities are heaped upon it, God's love keeps speaking through wet pages or dry.

It's a lot like Jesus. He suffered the storm of Calvary, was laid in a tomb, and declared gone. On the third day, with scars, He arose (1 Cor. 15:3-4). That's the heart of the gospel. He keeps on giving life—even to those who, through carelessness, almost lose Him but who find Him in time. Because of what He suffered, He is extremely precious to us who know Him.

The Lord and His Word are indestructible. Hallelujah!

Cleaned on Credit

Getting credit for somebody else's work. It happens.

Mark, nearly eleven, was visiting his grandparents. He needed some money and was willing to work for it. The shower stall needed cleaning, so the two needs were brought together. Grandma-ma would pay pretty good wages for the job, so the little scrubber cleaned it the best he could.

Papa happened to check the completed work before Grand-ma-ma did. It didn't look exactly like "Mr. Clean" had been there. Needed a little more elbow grease to make it shine. So Papa put the finishing touches to it.

Neither Grand-ma-ma nor Mark knew that phantom Papa had slipped in and out. So, a while later, after inspection, she told Mark what a fine job he had done and how good it looked. She put a bragging on him and he was paid for his work. He was real proud.

Papa was as silent as the night before Christmas about the whole affair. Not until sometime later did he let on as to what really happened. He wanted his work to be credited to his grandson's account.

The shower stall story reminds us of the showers of blessings God turns on His children.

A person's life can get pretty cruddy on the inside. Realizing he needs cleaning up, he "scrubs." Living better than he did, he feels pleased with himself. Folks around may even notice some improvement. But, alas, "All our righteousnesses are as filthy rags" (Isa. 64:6) in God's sight.

Then Jesus comes. He deep cleans us, for "the blood of Jesus Christ his Son cleanseth us from all sin" (1 John 1:7). Then wearing the robe of His righteousness, we sparkle. It's what God has done for us that counts. "Not by works of righteousness which we have done, but according to his mercy he saved us" (Titus 3:5) sets the record straight. The Bible calls it "imputed righteousness."

We may get congratulated for the obviously changed life, but inwardly, we know it was Jesus who sent the dirt down the drain. We merely cooperated with Him. We may get the credit, but He is the cause. The visible in us is there because of the work of the invisible Savior.

A "look-how-good-I-am" attitude is about as becoming to a recipient of God's cleansing grace as pride is to a pauper who thinks he worked for his unexpected inheritance.

It should be said of purified Christians by those who marvel at the change, "They [have] been with Jesus" (Acts 4:13).

Worth Cleaving To

The word *cleave* means to be glued to, to be stuck to, or to cling to. Some things can, ought, and should be cleaved to. The Bible uses this "sticky" word about important matters like marriage, our relationship with the Lord, and the goodies of life.

God says marriage makes man and woman so much a part of one another that they are one in His sight. Explaining this, He said, "Therefore shall a man leave his father and mother, and shall cleave unto his wife, and they two shall be one flesh" (Gen. 2:24).

Now it so happens that my wife's name is Harriett Cleaves. Many are the times she wondered why in the world she got a monicker like Cleaves. Mispronouncements and feeble joke attempts discomfited her at times during school years. Gladly would she have swapped Cleaves for something like Euodias or Syntyche—fine, solid Bible names (Phil. 4:2).

The Lord has ways of bringing good out of all things.

Time came when Harriett was right pleased with her double name. She even said she liked it. On our wedding invitations, the fancy engraving says, "Harriett Cleaves to the Reverend Crate Jones." You can bet your boots that that preacher is glad that she has, does, and from the looks of things, will, over thirty years already.

Turns out that cleaving is what God had in mind for folks who swap "I do's" at the altar. Jesus said, "What therefore God hath joined together, let not man put asunder" (Matt. 19:6). No matter what, married folks can cleave to each other like a miser holding onto his pocketbook, if they set their minds to it. It pleases the Lord mightily when folks cleave and keep cleaving.

Then again, God does something for those who cleave to Him. After routing Israel's foes, He said, "Ye that did cleave unto the Lord Your God are alive every one of you this day" (Deut. 4:4). They must've been glad they clove. Reminds us Christians that we are alive forever by cleaving to Jesus who wouldn't stop cleaving to the cross for us. Now we cleave to each other like the vine and the branch.

"Cleave to that which is good" (Rom. 12:9). That's what the Bible tells saved folks to do. We ought to love evil as much as we'd love to stroke a cottonmouth moccasin. Jesus lived good, saw good, did good. And He makes it possible for His people to do likewise.

Maybe more of us need Cleaves for our middle name. It might remind us to stick to things approved by the Lord.